Dior
haute couture Chanel
Paris
In fashion
miniskirt catwalk stiletto heel
embroidery prêt-à-porter

Dominique Paulvé
Marie Boyé

CASSELL&CO

5ft 9in (1m 76) Cindy Crawford
5ft 11in (1m 80) Claudia Schiffer
6ft (1m 83) Elle MacPherson.
The top models are extremely tall!  ▶ 86

The British textile and clothing industry produces **£14 billion** worth of goods. British designers sell more than **£650 million** worth of clothing at manufacturers' prices. In all, 270,000 people ▶ 84 are employed in the industry, 70% of whom are women.

The industry makes a significant contribution **to Britain's exports. Textiles and clothing together amount to the country's ninth biggest export. The main markets for British designers are the USA, Japan and Europe.**

(SOURCE: BRITISH FASHION COUNCIL) ▶ 110

3.5 million tonnes of nylon are made every year throughout the world. ▶ 96

The world *synthetic fibre industry* **continues to grow. In** *1999,* **at** *29.5 million* **tonnes, world output was** *1.2 million tonnes* **or** *4%* **higher than in the previous year. The same year, a fall in the price of cotton prompted an increase in the demand for** *natural fibres* **by** *1%.* **The share of the world fibre market now held by** *man-made fibres* **reached** *59%.* *Artificial fibres* **have brought about a revolution in price, fabric care, durability and comfort.**

 96

*Every year the House of Lesage in Paris uses **300** kg of beads and **100** million sequins.* ▶ 64

The future is bright for jobs in design. The stars are returning to haute couture, that much sought after art to which many are drawn, but few are chosen.

 72

From Paris to London by way of the big provincial cities, from Milan to New York by way of Tokyo, there are many major centres where you can learn the fashion business.

114

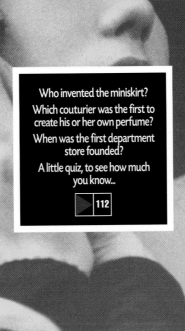

Who invented the miniskirt?

Which couturier was the first to create his or her own perfume?

When was the first department store founded?

A little quiz, to see how much you know...

▶ | 112

7

billion pairs of jeans were sold throughout the world in 1995. ▶ 98

Anything from nylon to Lycra, banana leaves to rubberised linen, even recycled plastic bottles, can be woven into a fabric, made into clothes, mixed together and decorated to produce unusual 'textiles' in this extraordinary modern age. The future of fashion is being shaped in laboratories, where new fabrics are born every day.

 96

One factory producing 150 tonnes of acrylic fibre per day can replace the wool produced by 12 million sheep; 150 tonnes of polyester fibre can be produced in one day to replace 100,000 hectares of cotton fields.

 96

It is becoming increasingly common for families who have kept their fine clothes for many years to donate them to museums all over the world, and curators buy pieces at auction in order to complete important collections.

▶ 117

An haute couture suit costs between £6,500 and £11,000; a prêt-à-porter suit £450; a mass-market suit £45.

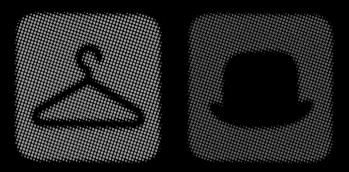

You can be a mad hatter, look for a needle in a haystack or talk through your hat... terms from within the clothing industry used in everyday speech.

 104

The Internet has caught on to this craze for anything to do with fashion: Web addresses...

 119

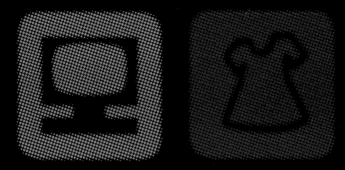

The process of creating a garment calls on many professions, combining creativity with production techniques.

 82

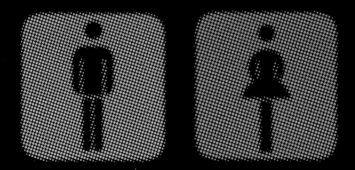

"Fashion is the sartorial expression of a given group of people at a precise moment in their history."
Bruno du Roselle

▶ 38

From the first fig leaf to the **garments** produced by **designers**, much has been written about dressing and undressing. Did people first wear clothes in order to conceal the **differences** between them, protect themselves from the heat or the cold, comply with the **laws** of religion or magic, or because of war? Ethnologists are still arguing about this. However, they have identified three **types** of garment: draped **costume**, a one-piece garment wrapped around the **body**; pull-on costume, a one-piece garment with a hole for the **head**; and **sewn** costume, made up of several **pieces** put together.

14

For each collection, Lesage, the Paris embroidery specialist, shows 250 to 300 samples of embroidery. A sample demands 40 to 60 hours' work and may contain as many as 100,000 stitches.

Embroidery is still widely practised in Britain, commercially and for pleasure. The Embroiderers' Guild has 2,400 full members.

In France, the home of haute couture, the demand for such clothes has fallen dramatically since the Second World War. In 1943, 20,000 women bought from designers, by 1990 the figure was just 200.

The discovery of nylon and new synthetic fibres brought about a revolution. In 1988 the production of synthetic fibres exceeded that of cotton for the first time. The sales of wool garments have fallen dramatically since the war, and continue to decline, dropping by 24% in the five years 1993–98.

In just one century, the average height of a man has increased by 8 cm (just over 3 in) and of a woman by 7 cm (just under 3 in).

DISCOVER

ONCE, STYLE WAS THE PRESERVE OF THE UPPER CLASSES, BUT INNOVATIONS
BROUGHT ABOUT BY THE INDUSTRIAL REVOLUTION IN THE 19TH CENTURY
MADE FASHIONABLE CLOTHING MORE AFFORDABLE. THE JOBS AND
TECHNIQUES OF TEXTILE PRODUCTION HAVE CONTINUED TO DEVELOP SO THAT,
AT THE BEGINNING OF THE 21ST CENTURY, THE GREATEST POSSIBLE NUMBER OF
PEOPLE HAVE ACCESS TO THE FASHION MARKET.

Since the world began, people have worn different clothes in order to keep warm or protect themselves from the sun, express their personality and proclaim their status. During the Stone Age, most of the European continent was covered by great glaciers. Cave dwellers soon learned to hunt animals not just for food but also for their fur, as protection against the cold. First they discovered how to chew the skins to make them supple, a procedure still practised by the Inuits, then they learned how to treat them with oil, cut them and sew them together.

Sometimes regarded as the earliest lady of fashion, the Dame de Brassempouy, a figurine made from mammoth ivory, was discovered by archaeologists in Stone Age deposits in the Landes region of south-west France. She is wearing a hat and has her hair bound in a net. This is the first known depiction of female headgear, which has varied enormously though the centuries.

DRESSMAKING: AN ANCIENT CRAFT

It was the nomadic peoples of the Neolithic Age who took the major step forward in using wool to make clothes, and when some of these people began to settle and form village communities they developed weaving of all kinds of hair and bark fibres. The ancient Egyptians invented trousers and linen loincloths, worn equally by men and women of high rank. Women generally covered their shoulders with a veil, and their social standing could be seen from their jewels and ruffs of beads and precious stones. Both sexes wore sandals made of papyrus or leather, but only on important occasions.

TUTANKHAMUN

Egypt, 17th Dynasty, around 1346–1337 BC. Relief on the tomb of Tutankhamun. Egyptian Museum, Cairo.

As for embroidery, it was mentioned by Pliny as early as 70 BC: 'The Phrygians invented the art of embroidering with a needle using gold and woollen thread. Babylon is famous for its coloured embroidery.' At first it was reserved for the clergy, then for kings and princes, and it reached its peak with the splendours of the court of the Sun King, Louis XIV. The first embroidery machine was invented in Mulhouse, France in 1829.

Artificial flowers were also made in ancient times. They were used to decorate chariots and the entrances to houses, and by Chinese ladies to decorate their hair. With the associated professions of plumassier and milliner, flower makers were officially recognised in France in 1776, and given the title of *maîtres* or *maîtresses fleuristes* – master florists. The most famous of these were Italian. The Italians were also acknowledged as the best at making gold braid in the 13th century, and many moved to France in the 14th century to pass on their expertise. Ribbon's popularity reached its height in Europe in the 17th and 18th centuries. It had pretensions to being a precious commodity, and was even the subject of much-coveted gifts. The fortunes of the city of Coventry, which had been in decline in the 16th century, were revived largely through the establishment of silk ribbon manufacture there in the 17th century.

CONCERN OVER THE DANGERS OF CORSETS

Corsets first appeared in the 12th century, but until the 15th century they were made and worn only by men. From the 14th to the 16th century, women began to adopt them, worn as a bodice over the dress and laced at the front. In the 18th century some doctors started to voice their worries about the dangers of tight lacing, a controversy which reached its height at the turn of the 20th century. The corset is perhaps the most extreme example of a garment being used to change body shape, but there have been many others. In 1340, men wore the padded doublet, covered by a houppelande (cloak), which was often made of fur. Around the same time, Poland introduced the pointed poulaine shoe. The codpiece, a sign of virility that had been introduced from Switzerland and Germany, became bigger and bigger by stuffing it with handkerchiefs, money and sweets. Hats reached monumental proportions in the years leading up to the end of the 15th century, when ladies wore the cumbersome steeple-hat or hennin. At various times, panniers, farthingales and crinolines have been used to give bulk and shape to skirts.

'FASHION' BEGINS IN THE 14TH CENTURY

It is difficult to precisely date the birth of fashion. Throughout the ages men and women have considered the way they dressed, and copied other people's styles. According to the Oxford dictionary, the use of the term 'fashion' to describe dress is first recorded at the turn of the 17th

ALEXANDER, DUKE OF PARMA

Padded doublet, covered by a houppelande. Painting by S. Anguisciola (1535–1625), National Gallery of Arts, Dublin.

century. However, the increased use of decorative features in clothing, and the greater attention paid to the cut of garments and the materials from which they were made as early as the 14th century are perhaps a more accurate indication of the arrival of the fashion phenomenon. Since then, Western fashion has been generally dictated by France, but at different periods, other countries have been major influences.

A BREATH OF AUSTERITY

Silk and velvet grew in popularity in the 16th century, made into embroidered jackets called casaques, worn over hauts-de-chausse, and doublets with slashes in every possible colour. The square neckline became the accepted fashion for women, with an embroidered gorget and a high goffered collar. With the ascendancy of Spain in Europe in the mid-16th century, when Mary Tudor married the Spanish King Philip II, black was introduced into men's costume, which was soberly embroidered and covered by a cape. Women's costume also became more austere. Dark-coloured gowns with padded sleeves were worn over a well-stiffened bodice and a farthingale, with a white fraise or ruff, at the neck. The relative severity of Spanish styles even had its effect at the French court, and Henry IV, proclaiming his taste for simplicity, banned the import of rich fabrics and useless fripperies. However, lace remained in fashion, used in starched collars for men and for women, who wore layered skirts and laced bodices with voluminous sleeves.

THE MYSTERIES OF LACE AND LACEMAKING

The origins of lacemaking are still the subject of dispute. Homer's passionate descriptions of veils placed by Helen on the knees of the goddess Minerva seem to indicate that they were made of a form of lace, but it is more likely that the lacemaking profession originated in Venice in the second half of the 16th century. From this time, lace became an indispensable accessory for men and women, and both sexes wore ruffs in place of collars. The ruffs worn by Queen Elizabeth I were particularly elaborate.

NEW FASHIONS IN FRANCE UNDER THE SUN KING

The reign of Louis XIV, the Sun King, was characterised by every kind of extravagance, and by this time Paris was calling the tune for all the capitals of Europe. From Germany to England, miles of ribbon and lace were used to decorate men's short, buttoned doublets and the wide rhinegrave (or petticoat) breeches. Buttons, which existed as long ago as the 3rd millennium BC, and first appeared on garments at the end of the 12th century, became an established item on the long jackets now in fashion. Made by goldsmiths from bone, horn, or ivory, they were precious objects.

FEATHERS, RIBBONS, EMBROIDERY: SOPHISTICATION IS THE RULE

Moroccan leather was unknown before the 17th century, but we know that in the Middle Ages purses made from deerskin, horsehide, pigskin and cowhide were worn on the belt. Travellers' bags and packs and other everyday objects were also fashioned from these materials. The sophistication of the 18th century made lizard, crocodile and ostrich skin fashionable. The *veste*, the forerunner of the waistcoat, appeared at the end of the Sun King's reign. Men wore long wigs and carried felt hats overburdened with feathers in their hands.

PLUMASSIER AND EMBROIDERER

Plate from the Encyclopaedia of Diderot and Alembert.

Women were a little less conspicuous. Above the corset laced tight around their waists, they wore Venice or Flanders lace to fill in the deep décolletage, where they would place silk patches which sometimes had esoteric significance. Wide skirts, decorated with embroidery and braid, were gathered up over stiff petticoats. Their elaborate hairstyles were absolutely laden with ribbons and lace. Rose Bertin, Marie-Antoinette's dressmaker, put feathers everywhere she could! Working with feathers, which had adorned hats since the Middle Ages, had been solely a man's preserve. The art was so specialised that it took six years' apprenticeship and four years as a guild

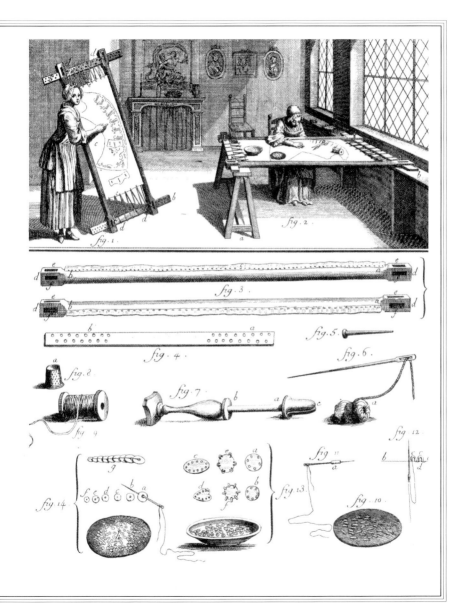

fig. 1.

fig. 2.

fig. 3.

fig. 4.

fig. 5.

fig. 6.

fig. 7.

fig. 8.

fig. 9.

fig. 10.

fig. 11.

fig. 12.

fig. 13.

fig. 14.

member before you were allowed to practise the profession. Peacock feathers were the first to be used, followed in the 14th century by ostrich, then cock, goose, vulture, pheasant and jay. The first guild of plumassiers, founded in 1577, also included flower-makers and embroiderers.

THE AGE OF PANNIERED SKIRTS

In both interior decoration and clothing, the 18th century had a passion for everything Chinese and Indian, and all kinds of embroidered motifs brought back from the colonies. Around 1705 dresses became lighter and flounced, then about ten years later they were draped over bell-shaped panniers. Corsets were pointed and laced up the back. Delicate pieces of lace-edged sleeves, the same fabric used as for the *modestie* filling in the low neckline. Fur-lined pelisses were worn throughout the century. Men wore justaucorps, breeches, jackets and the lace jabot, which was the forerunner of the tie.

Around 1770, the pannier was replaced by the smaller 'tournure', and bodices pushed the bust higher. At about the same time, the 'redingote' (a French corruption of the English words 'riding coat') dress was introduced. But the main interest was centred on hairstyles. Small, curly chignons were quickly followed by curled hair worn high on the head and decorated with ribbons and lace. Bonnets then took over, until finally the hairstyles of fashionable ladies were adorned with floral arrangements, vegetables and bizarre objects of all kinds.

NOBLE GERMAN COUPLE

He wears breeches and a jabot. She wears a dress with panniers and a hat with a floral arrangement. Circa 1780.

The French Revolution brought major changes in fashion throughout Europe: 'court dress' disappeared in favour of a simple, fluid style inspired by English country life. Cut from lightweight fabrics, preferably white and high-waisted, these flimsy dresses were sometimes so transparent that it was necessary to wear flesh-coloured 'tights' (an early all-in-one alternative to stockings underneath). Motifs copied from cashmere shawls were printed on silk, percale, muslin and cotton.

FASHIONABLE LADIES WEAR THE PERFUMES OF THE ENGLISH COUNTRYSIDE

After 1825, the high waists began to get lower, and the straight, narrow lines gradually became fuller. England began to dictate fashion, and the dandies took an English style of elegance to Paris. Woollen fabrics were all the rage. Women were soon wearing spencers over longer, full skirts. The dramatic crinoline appeared about 1845, and remained popular until the end of the 1860s. What had started as a simple petticoat stiffened with horsehair became a large framework of hoops, and this was adopted by the Empress Eugénie, consort of Napoléon III, as a tribute to Marie-Antoinette.

RECOGNITION FOR DRESSMAKERS

During the 19th century, women of the growing middle class, who until then had made their own clothes, began to call on the services of professionals, giving rise to dressmaking as a women's profession. Until this time, the activity had mostly been the preserve of men, although there had been women dressmakers as far back as the 17th century. Now they were described as 'dressmakers and cutters' and their task was to cut, sew, decorate and finish garments. This brought them into competition with both the master tailors and the second-hand clothes dealers. The wealthiest people called in jobbing dressmakers, who reproduced the designs from the fashion-plates published in popular women's magazines.

THE 19TH CENTURY: THE BIRTH OF THE CLOTHING INDUSTRY

Certain kinds of loom had existed since ancient times to produce fabrics, but it was not until the late 18th century that anything like mass manufacture was possible. Two of the significant early events in the Industrial Revolution were James Hargreaves' invention of the spinning jenny and Sir Richard Arkwright's invention of the spinning frame, and, at the beginning of the 19th century, Joseph-Marie Jacquard perfected the loom to which he gave his name.

A few years later, in 1830, Barthélémy Thimonnier invented the sewing machine (thimbles and metal needles had been in existence since 1370). The clothing industry, a term which covers all the activities relating to the mass production of garments, was born. It was at this time that dress-designers first appeared, and their role was not only to make clothes but also to sell them. This new area of activity enabled thousands of people to earn a living.

MANUFACTURING
Sewing the fabric for umbrellas. The factory of Léon-Lafarge and family, Angers.

The demand for military uniforms and special clothing for particular professions made a major contribution to the expansion of the clothing industry, which was closely linked to economic and industrial upheavals, as well as the growth of the working classes. Clothes were expensive in the cities, and, unlike country folk, townspeople did not barter them for goods. So, to make prices as low as possible, clothing manufacturers produced costume which was, to say the least, very simple and rudimentary. For men, it was reduced to straight trousers, a long, loose jacket, and a shirt with a detachable collar. Women's clothing, inspired by regional costumes, was composed of a long, gathered skirt, and a full white blouse tucked in at the waist. Dressmakers and tailors were brought together in big factories, but ready-made garments remained extremely simple until the big department stores encouraged the creation of new, more attractive outfits.

THE FIRST SEWING MACHINE

Invented by Thimonnier in 1830

THE BIG DEPARTMENT STORES: LOW PRICES BUT A WIDE CHOICE

Department stores appeared in the mid-19th century, initially catering essentially for the working class, who were at last able to choose between several designs of clothing. The very first store was developed from a shop opened in 1838 by Emerson Muschamp Bainbridge with draper William Dunn in Newcastle upon Tyne. By 1849 it had been divided into 32 departments, and was selling dress and furnishing fabrics, fashion accessories, furs and family mourning, as well as made-up muslin dresses – the first, primitive examples of ready-to-wear clothing. Bon Marché was founded by Aristide Boucicaut in Paris in 1852. It was originally solely a haberdashery shop, but in the 1870s expanded to encompass a wide range of departments. The 1860s in London saw the opening of John Lewis's shop in Oxford Street, and the expansion of Dickins & Jones and Swan & Edgar, which now included a suite of showrooms for displaying fashions. The principle of being able to exchange purchases was introduced in some stores, and prices were kept low because the large quantity of garments sold compensated for the small profit made on each article. The clothing industry's mission was to improve the dress of an increasingly large clientele, while that of haute couture was to dress the elite.

CHARLES FREDERICK WORTH: THE FIRST 'GRAND COUTURIER'

It was through the patronage of the Empress Eugénie of France that Charles Frederick Worth, a young fabric salesman from Lincolnshire, became a fashion star. His magisterial look and his talent for cutting, coupled with the speed at which the clothes were made, charmed the ladies who found the usual process of undergoing six fittings extremely tiring. In 1858, at the height of the Second Empire, he opened his own shop in the rue de la Paix in Paris. The Empress, who ordered all her ball gowns from him, nicknamed him the 'tyrant of fashion' because of his irascible nature and insolent despotism. Worth was a natural innovator, and one of the first couturiers to use machine sewing for the inner seams of garments. He also had lace and embroidery machines built, prepared his own dyes, and labelled his designs. His magnificent crinolined skirts swung like a bell from a woman's waist, and revealed her boots, giving impetus to developments in fashions for footware.

EARLY 20TH CENTURY

Advertisement for the fashion department of Bon Marché, 1915.

Another Englishman who made his mark in Paris was Charles Redfern. Born in a draper's shop on the Isle of Wight, Redfern owed his notoriety to the sporty, personal way he dressed English yachtsmen. Although he was primarily a man's tailor, he invented the 'Prince of Wales' suit for Alexandra, the Princess of Wales, and it was an immediate success. In 1881, he set up in Paris, with the emphasis on severe, elegant suits and riding clothes with a sporty, feminine look.

JACQUES DOUCET: A TASTE FOR LIGHTNESS

Around 1885, Jacques Doucet opened a couture department in his parents' lingerie shop. He was an aesthete, drawing inspiration from the works of contemporary and controversial artists. His clothes were not conceived with the idea of following the fashion of a particular season, but rather they were worked out according to the physique, hair colour and complexion of his clients. For the ethereal kind of woman he loved to dress, he chose layers of muslin, voile, gauze,

PIERROT COSTUME
*Costume for a
fancy-dress ball, 1914.*

tulle or lawn. He had huge quantities of lace, which was the family speciality, made for his ball gowns. Lucile (Lady Duff Cooper) began dressmaking in the 1890s and a year later opened her first salon in London. In the first two decades of the 20th century, she was widely respected as a designer, with branches in New York, Chicago and Paris. She created clothes for the dancer Irene Castle, Sarah Bernhardt, film stars and royalty, and in 1907 designed costumes for the London premiere of Lehár's *The Merry Widow*.

From the moment she set up in business in 1893, Jeanne Paquin was admired for her suit designs, her meticulous detail, and a particular shade of red, which she included in all her collections. She used an abundance of lace, treated fur as if it were a fabric, and made use of contrasting materials. She was a formidable businesswoman, and had a taste for the avant-garde, ordering sketches for dresses from artists such as Léon Bakst.

PAUL POIRET PUTS FASHION INTO SHOP WINDOWS

Paul Poiret revolutionised fashion with his loose-fitting kimonos and the exotic, flowing garments he designed for the dancer Isadora Duncan. With these clothes, he claimed to have 'liberated women from their corsets'. He was certainly the most innovative couturier in the 20th century. He was the first to display his dresses in a shop window, to make trousers for women, to create a perfume and to link couture with interior decoration by setting up the École Martine. The latter employed untrained young women who designed textiles and furnishings to be made up later by skilled craftsmen. Poiret was the first to ask artists like Raoul Dufy to design fabrics, and to organise a fashion show circuit in Europe. Inspired by Bakst's oriental designs for the Ballets Russes, he featured turbans, aigrettes (high-plumed feathers) and harem pants.

Jeanne Lanvin started out as a milliner, but opened her first couture house in 1909. Her clothes were characterised by their elegance, the fabulous embroidery on her evening wear, and the creation of the 'Lanvin blue', which she took from medieval stained glass windows. She also expressed her talent in the areas of (interior) decoration and in perfumery, and was the first to open a men's department in a couture house, which she named Monsieur Lanvin.

H.Robert Dammy

MADELEINE VIONNET'S OBSESSION WITH BIAS

Another Doucet graduate, Madeleine Vionnet, made her appearance in 1912, and from the start impertinently ignored customs and fashion. She pursued her obsession with folding fabrics on the bias and further refining the art of draping, twisting and rolling the material until she achieved the absolute perfection of classical statues. Fortunately she was able to dress daring women, who were proud of their bodies and had no hesitation about wearing skin-tight clothing. She was soon dubbed the 'geometrician of couture'. In order to achieve the famous bias, she had an enormous loom built, so big that a hole had to be made in the workshop ceiling in order to accommodate it.

After one or two fruitless attempts, Jean Patou opened his couture house in 1919. The post-war emancipation of women helped them to be taken seriously for the first time in competitive sport, and Patou recognised this, inventing the concept of sportswear in 1922. He was advised by the tennis player Suzanne Lenglen, for whom he created the calf-length pleated skirt that caused such a sensation. This was a garment for wearing on and off court, bringing fashion into sport, and projecting women as sports personalities.

Edward Henry Molyneux was born in London in 1894, and began his career in the fashion industry by sketching for advertisements and magazines. In 1911, his design for an evening dress won him first prize in a competition set by Lucile, and she later employed him as a sketcher in her salon. Molyneux opened his own house in Paris in 1919, where during the First World War he invented the *pyjama du soir*, the three-quarter length coat, and, later on, a suit with a soft jacket that became popular all over the world. In the 1930s, he promoted the 'little black dress', along with Chanel. Despite these innovations, for Molyneux the most important thing was the quality of his fabrics.

COCO CHANEL INVENTS THE SUIT

**COCO CHANEL
(1883–1971)**

*Surrounded by models
in her Paris flat.*

Already known for her hat designs, Coco Chanel opened her first couture house in Deauville, the playground of the rich, in 1913, then one in Biarritz, and finally one in Paris in 1920. Her simple, straight dresses and wool jersey suits made every other outline seem old-fashioned. This expression of freedom spread to her clients; they wore short hair, berets, and dresses which clung to their bodies. In 1936 she produced her first 'little black dress', and three years later, beach trousers. All her life, Chanel was surrounded by artists and stage and screen personalities. The jewels she wore and designed became famous, as did the wide trousers inspired by men's fashions. Her sumptuous evening dresses were covered in embroidery. In the 1950s, when her fashion house reopened following the war, pride of place went to a garment which won her international success: the *petit tailleur* (little suit). Since 1983, Karl Lagerfeld, as design director for the Chanel house, has perpetuated her image, albeit very much in his own way.

In 1925, under the banner of youth, Marcel Rochas set up his first salon, showing sensible, feminine, tasteful clothes. He liked white, piqué collars showing above the suit jacket, wide trousers, and coats inspired by men's overcoats. Later he was to make a great deal of use of lace, both for his evening dresses and for the guêpière or 'waspie' corset, which he created in homage to the curvaceous figure of Mae West, and which paved the way for Dior's 'New Look'.

Elsa Schiaparelli was born in Rome and moved to Paris in 1920, aged 30. One of her first designs was a black sweater with a white bow knitted into it, giving a trompe l'oeil effect. She liked to amuse, by wit or through shock tactics. Incorporated in her garments were zips, part of the design rather than purely functional and coloured to co-ordinate with the fabrics. She also used padlocks on suits. Schiaparelli became noted for her use of colour, particularly 'shocking pink', invented by the painter and set designer Christian Bérard.

READY-TO-WEAR STEALS A MARCH ON HAUTE COUTURE

Spurred on by the success of haute couture in the 1920s, the big department stores attempted to increase their clientele. When they were hit by the slump in 1929, they were forced to lower their prices considerably. In Paris, the Monoprix and Prisunic stores made their appearance, selling goods all at 'one price'. Lowering prices implies large-scale manufacturing, and while it was possible to produce bigger quantities more cheaply and to improve the quality, variety suffered in consequence. Fortunately, the world of haute couture came to the rescue, and couturiers began to create clothes that could be worn by working women as well as by a select few. Coco Chanel introduced a new, boyish silhouette, the *garçonne*, characterised by its simple shape and using only small amounts of fabric. This line became the model for industrial producers. From then on, the ready-to-wear sector of the industry drew inspiration from haute couture designs in order to define the style for mass-produced garments.

FASHION SKETCHES
From Harper's Bazaar, 1938. Designs by Molyneux, Alix and Paquin. Victoria & Albert Museum, London.

CRISTOBAL BALENCIAGA: SIMPLE BUT INIMITABLE LINES

After escaping his home country's civil war, the Spaniard Cristobal Balenciaga presented his first Paris collection in August 1937. A short item in a professional journal, noting his very original way of making a sleeve, was enough to bring buyers flocking to his premises in the avenue George V. Women adored his sober lines, his inimitable little black dresses and his impeccably cut suits,

On these pages, indisputable evidence that Paris is plaid-mad.

Molyneux. A tight little
jacket and a deep-pleated skirt

Alix. A plaid blouse under
a mulberry suit, and over
all an off-white coat

Paquin's dark brown
antelope sports coat
lined with plaid

Also at Alix, a great coat
of rainbow plaid with all
the fulness swept to the front

which attracted attention at the races. To his Paris colleagues he quickly became known as 'The Master'. This unusual couturier became a legend for his strictness, as well as his capacity for work and his extraordinary technique. He invented the sack dress in 1950, the chemise in 1957, the baby-doll, the kimono sleeve in 1959, and he relaunched the fashion for saris.

WARTIME RESTRICTIONS: ROOM FOR THE IMAGINATION!

The onset of the Second World War meant that fabric was rationed. Just before the war, there had been signs that fashion designers were opting for more extravagant use of cloth in dresses, and there had even been the suggestion of the return of crinoline. But such excesses had to be put on hold, and women were forced to adopt a more severe form of clothing. British government instructions demanded a more utilitarian approach to dress. From 1942, a man was entitled to buy an overcoat once every seven years, a pullover every five years, a pair of trousers and a jacket every two years, a pair of underpants every two years, a shirt every 20 months and a pair of shoes every eight months. Restrictions for women were similarly severe. The effect of

DURING THE SECOND WORLD WAR

As stockings were no longer available, women painted their legs with walnut stain and even drew seams in pencil.

this was not really felt until about two years later, when existing clothes began to show serious signs of wear and tear. A 'Make Do And Mend' campaign, in which people were exhorted to adapt old clothes, and the introduction of harder-wearing utility clothes improved matters slightly, but morale was distinctly suffering.

In Paris, war and then the occupation were devastating for the couturiers, who were allowed just three metres to make a dress. They rivalled one another in imagination, creating dresses that could be transformed by adding a flounce for visits to the theatre, smocks which could be worn over the same basic dress, culotte-skirts for cycling, and accessories borrowed from interior decorators' shops. The industry kept going, thanks partly to a few ingenious Frenchwomen, who managed to find fabrics despite the war, and particularly to the wives and mistresses of the German officers and collaborators, to whom the couturiers were obliged to sell from time to time in order to prevent their businesses from being closed. The Germans had planned to move the Paris fashion centre to Vienna or Berlin, but the determination of the Haute Couture Employers' Federation put a stop to this project.

The designer Alix, who had become known in 1934 for her beachwear and her drapes using new textures, opened a salon during the war under the name of Grès, where she showed dresses in blue, white and red, the colours of the French flag. The Nazi authorities reacted immediately, ordering the business to be closed, but she opened again in 1942. This 'grande dame' of haute couture, who wanted to be a sculptor, created a new kind of peplum (a classical sleeveless gown) for seamless silk jersey dresses made from extra-wide fabrics woven specially for her.

THE POSTWAR PERIOD: THE COUTURIERS REOPEN THEIR DOORS

When she opened her fashion house in Jean Patou's former studio on the Champs-Elysées, Carven had two precise objectives: to dress young women in simple, practical fashions, and to cater for women like herself, who were ignored by haute couture because they were less than 5 ft 3 in (1 m 60 cm) tall. Whereas her colleagues would present one wedding dress at the end of a collection, Carven would show ten at the start of the parade. She liked cheerful shades and her lucky colour was green. She excelled at getting the best out of what had hitherto been considered a disadvantage, so short women at last felt valued.

Pierre Balmain also came on the scene in 1945, opening his fashion house with long, bell-shaped skirts and small waists. He had worked for Molyneux in the 1930s, and then for the Lelong studio, where he had met Christian Dior. Smart upper-class women liked Balmain's sober, structured style, the narrow waists contrasting with wide coats. He had particular success in the USA with his ready-to-wear clothes, through his ability to translate French fashion into outfits for American women with their generally larger frames.

The year 1947 was marked by Christian Dior's first collection, on a theme called 'Corolle' in French, but known in England as the 'New Look', with wasp waists and full skirts. Dior reacted against the restrictions imposed by the war, lowering hemlines to within a foot of the ground and using thirty metres of fabric for the most important dress in the show, which was inspired by the elegance of the Second Empire. The New Look was roundly condemned in Britain by the future prime minister Harold Wilson, then president of the Board of Trade, who made himself very unpopular with women by demanding a continuation of the austerity in fashion imposed during the war. Dior's worldwide success began with the famous 'Bar' suit, which established the fashionable silhouette of the time. During his short career, he launched perfumes and shops, and dressed women from head to toe, with hats by Claude Saint-Cyr and shoes by Roger Vivier.

YVES SAINT-LAURENT
In offices located on the first floor of 65 Rue de la Boétie in Paris, Saint-Laurent sketches a design on a sheet of glass.

The early 1950s saw the arrival of two young designers who were also to make their mark. Hubert de Givenchy's co-ordinated ensembles were a great success. He produced ready-to-wear clothes under his Nouvelle Boutique label. Pierre Cardin worked on costume design for Jean Cocteau's film *Beauty and the Beast*, and went on to open his own fashion house in 1953. His refined coats and suits made a particular impact. When Dior died in 1957, his young assistant, Yves Saint Laurent briefly took over and then opened his own house in 1961. Later, in 1966, he launched the first of a series of ready-to-wear boutiques, a trend that many were to follow.

THE HEPCATS: A TASTE FOR PROVOCATION

Towards the end of the war, a new movement was starting among young people in Paris – the *zazous* or 'hepcats'. The men wore checked jackets, fitted at the waist and reaching down to their knees, wide trousers, mustard-coloured socks and heavy shoes with huge built-up soles. Their hair was long, completing a look that carried with it more than a hint of provocation. The girls' uniform consisted of short skirts and polo-neck jumpers, with sheepskin jackets on top, and shoulder bags were an absolute must. Nicknamed *les incroyables de l'occupation* (the weirdos of the occupation), they reacted against the wartime restrictions with a craving for jazz and swing. It was the first time this sort of youth movement had been seen in France, and it had its echoes across the Channel in England. The teddy-boys (and girls) of the mid-1950s were so-named because they wore mock-Edwardian fashions, with long drape jackets often in bright colours, tight narrow trousers, thick crepe-soled shoes, and long sideboards. Again, their uniform and behaviour were a reaction to the austerity of rationing, which continued for many years after the war.

PRÊT-À-PORTER: A WHOLE PROCESSION OF IDEAS

Following the war, the concept of 'ready-to-wear', rechristened 'prêt-à-porter', invaded France from America. Its first official appearance was in 1947, in the report of the Congrès de l'Industrie du Vêtement Feminin, and the firm of Weill began using the term in their advertising in 1951. The prêt-à-porter industry offered moderately priced garments, cut and sewn on a production line, in a wide range of sizes. At the same time, the couturiers were trying to reach a wider clientele, so in 1950, on the initiative of Jean Gaumont-Lanvin, five big Parisian designers (Jean Dessès, Carven, Paquin, Jacques Fath and Robert Piguet) got together with seven clothing manufacturers to create seven comparatively modestly priced designs, for which they would still receive royalties. Others, such as Dior, Balenciaga, Yves Saint Laurent, André Courrèges and Pierre Cardin, later followed into the mass-distribution market.

VERSACE
Haute couture, spring 2000, models stride forth along the catwalk.

NEW PROFESSIONS GROW UP AROUND PRÊT-À-PORTER

The prêt-à-porter trade was a favourable environment for the emergence of brands such as Cacharel, Calvin Klein and Sonia Rykiel, and the birth of a new form of retail distribution – boutiques. These first flourished in London, where Mary Quant opened Bazaar as early as 1955 and Barbara Helinki started Biba in 1964. Fashion magazines, such as *Vogue, Elle,* and *Marie-Claire,* carried articles about the new products and were active participants in the success of mass-produced clothing. In an attempt to integrate the concept of fashion within their collections, the manufacturers of the 1960s recognised the need for designers within their industry. Sometimes taking their cue from haute couture, but often stimulating new trends, it was the job of these designers to produce the first models for manufacturers. Fashion advisers and trend consultants for the fashion industry also emerged because of prêt-à-porter. They began by working for the big stores that produced their own collections and then gradually gained their independence and set up offices of their own to serve the manufacturers. The first trend consultancy firm was opened by Maïmé Arnodin in 1960. Prêt-à-porter also required fashion buyers, product managers, merchandisers and other professions not previously associated with the clothing industry, and directly linked to selling through boutiques and specialist retailers.

DESIGN 1960–1970

As a result of the baby boom, by 1965 10 per cent of the world population was under twenty years old. For these new consumers clothes became a means of self-expression, and fashion split up into a multitude of styles, to a large part influenced by teenage rebellion.

HANAE MORI
*Flight of butterflies,
Haute couture show,
summer 1996.*

Since the early 1960s, every few years has seen the birth of a new 'tribe' – mods and rockers, hippies, skinheads, punks, rastas, new romantics, grunge and rave fans – each with their own specific style of dress and way of behaving. Possessing a language all of its own, fashion mirrors the everyday life of a given period and society in perpetual evolution.

With a simplified silhouette, and accessories made exclusively by the couturier, André Courrèges and Paco Rabanne gave the women of 1965 a total look. Courrèges' delicate pastel shades contrasted sharply with Rabanne's chainmail dresses, put together with pliers instead of needles, and metal discs and loops instead of fabric. In the same year, Emmanuel Ungaro made his name with his mixtures of prints. Jean-Charles de Castelbajac presented his first collection in 1970 with a coat that is still famous, made from his boarding-school blanket. He has used a whole range of unusual fabrics in his designs, such as cloth normally used for cleaning floors, waxed cotton and the sort of fur fabric used for making soft toys. Thierry Mugler's *collection spectacle* of 1977, featured padded shoulders and introduced 'sidereal blue'.

FRENCH DOMINATION ENRICHED BY FOREIGN TALENT

France continues to dominate fashion, but Italy has proclaimed its status as a design centre since the 1950s, when Emilio Pucci's dresses and designs in intense colours captivated the French. Everyone was wearing his simple, close-fitting, silk jersey dresses, belted at the waist with a little

cord ending in a glass pendant. He was to be followed by Nino Cerruti with his fluid fabrics in 1967, Giorgio Armani with his timeless suits in 1975 and Gianni Versace with his designs for sensual women, presented in Paris in 1982.

Japanese couturiers took Paris by surprise in 1970, with Kenzo's flowers in his first boutique 'Jungle Jap'. In 1972 Issey Miyake, who was steeped in the traditions of his own country, presented clothes which were very free in their cut, rather like kimonos. In 1977, Hanae Mori let her flight of butterflies loose on Paris, and the following year Yohji Yamamoto arrived with 'the tranquillity of dark colours'. Close on their heels came Rei Kawakubo (Comme des Garçons) with her full, torn, unfinished garments. The Groupe des Six, an association of young Belgian designers (including Dries van Noten) from the Royal Academy of Fine Arts in Antwerp, came to prominence in Paris in 1982. From then on, the fashion industry began to look towards the rest of the world, and the landscape of couture was enriched by Swiss, Turkish, Korean and Dutch designers.

THE BRITISH ARE COMING

Since the mid-19th century, British couturiers have been drawn to Paris, and continue to be so. John Galliano took over as creative director at Dior in 1996, and Alexander McQueen was appointed head designer at Givenchy the same year. Galliano, whose extravagant and highly original designs have been astounding people ever since his degree show in 1984, is inspired by the past, as Dior himself was. His designs consciously reflect a desire to emulate the New Look the 1940s, with the hour-glass figure. McQueen is considered something of a wild man of fashion, supposedly terrorising the employees in his workshops, and using accessories made from animal skin and bone. At one point he presented designs in homage to the British workman's 'bum cleavage'.

Other British couturiers have made their mark in recent years, although they have not felt it necessary to move to Paris to achieve success. Vivienne Westwood had virtually no training for her career, having spent just one term at Harrow Art School before leaving to train as a teacher. In the 1960s, she opened a shop with Malcolm McLaren on London's Kings Road, which eventually became the centre of punk fashion. She also promoted the 'pirate' and 'new romantic' looks of huge swirling petticoats, buckles, ruffles, pirate hats and baggy boots. Zandra Rhodes trained in textile printing and lithography, and began her career by designing her own highly individual fabrics, which she then made into dresses for sale at a shop in London. She showed her first dress collection in 1969, and became noted for her unique method of combining texture and pattern. Paul Smith has made a name for himself with men's fashions, originally produced in his home city of Nottingham, and his business still has its headquarters there. From a small shop in an alleyway in 1970, Smith has now built up a business with a multimillion pound turnover.

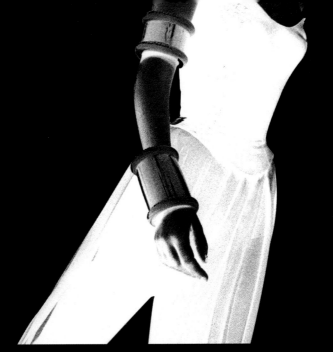

LOOK

BACKSTAGE AT A FASHION SHOW. EXCITEMENT, INTIMACY.
THE ADRENALIN RUSH. LAST MINUTE ADJUSTMENTS FROM
THE MAKE-UP ARTIST OR THE HAIRDRESSER AND A FINAL
TWEAK OF A FOLD FROM THE DESIGNER, AND... YOU'RE ON!

Jean-Paul Gaultier.

Isabelle Marant.

Yves Saint Laurent.

José Lévy.

Yves Saint Laurent.

Olivier Theyskens.

Jean-Paul Gaultier.

Christian Lacroix.

Olivier Theyskens.

Christian Lacroix.

Yves Saint Laurent.

Olivier Theyskens.

AF. Vandervorst.

Jean-Paul Gaultier.

Valentin Yudashkin.

A. Herchcovitch.

Gianfranco Ferré.

Thierry Mugler.

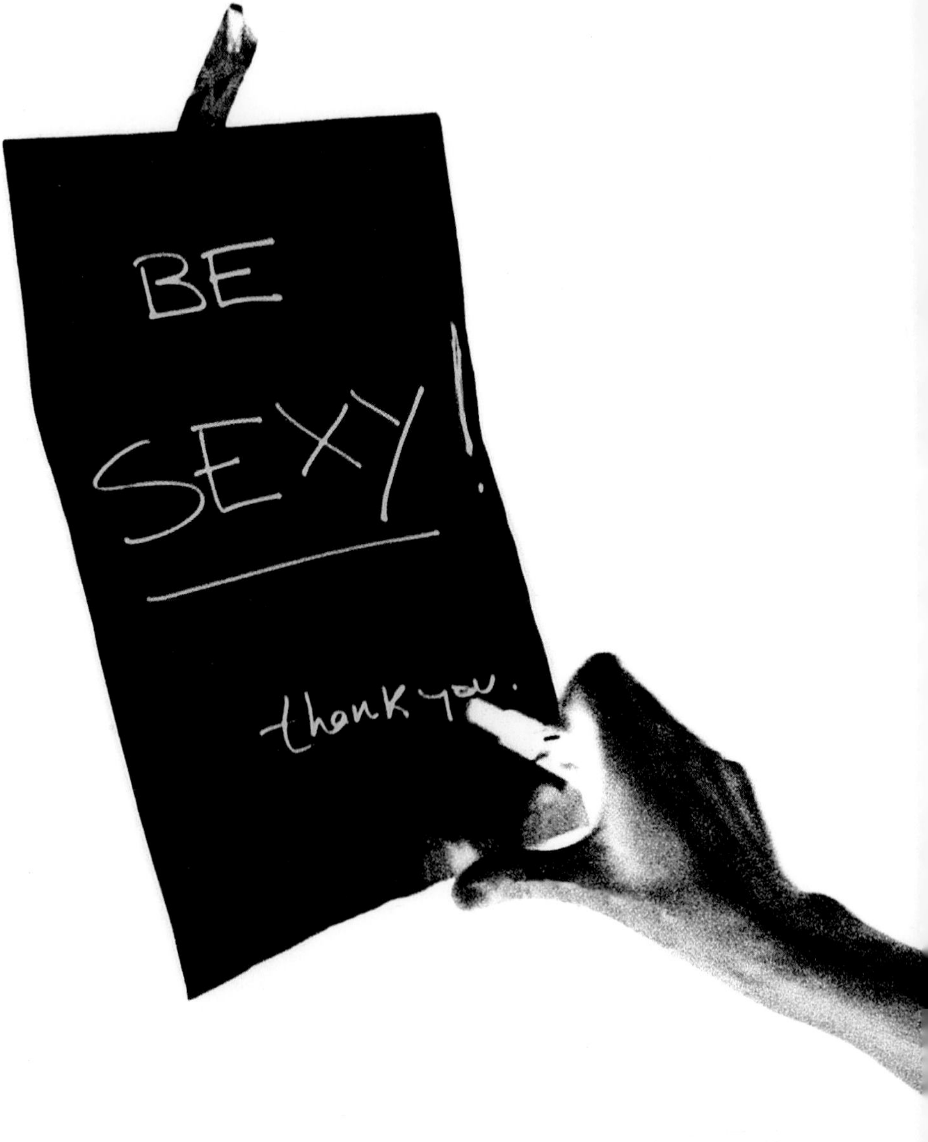
BE
SEXY!
thank you.

IN PRACTICE

THERE ARE A RANGE OF JOBS AND PROFESSIONS ASSOCIATED WITH THE FASHION INDUSTRY. IN THE RAREFIED WORLD OF PARISIAN HAUTE COUTURE, SOME PROFESSIONS ARE EXTREMELY SPECIALISED, WHEREAS MOST PEOPLE WORKING WITH THESE SKILLS IN BRITAIN WILL NEED TO COMBINE THEM WITH OTHERS. ALL THE PROFESSIONS NEED SPECIALIST TRAINING AND SUITABLE EXPERTISE. WHICH JOB IS FOR YOU?

Fashion industry skills: embroiderer, lacemaker and corsetière

Embroidery can be worked by hand or machine. The hand-made embroidery associated with haute couture consists of using a needle or a crochet hook to reproduce a design with thread on a fabric. Paillettes or beads or other ornamental features, such as small pieces of wood or metal, may be added. The motifs are drawn out beforehand on a toile. Then the design is transferred to the fabric, which may be anything from tulle, velvet or raffia to the bark of the banana tree! The tools and materials – presser-foot, soap, atomiser, pounce, lead weight, spray gun, dye – are carefully prepared, the threads counted, the paillettes weighed out. Then the work can begin. There are many embroidery stitches to choose from: satin stitch, stem stitch, buttonhole stitch, herringbone stitch, backstitch, couching, point de Lunéville, point de Beauvais... Different stitches require different implements – a crochet hook is used for chain stitch and its derivatives, Lunéville stitch or Beauvais stitch for example. Machine embroidery has been in existence since 1829, when Josua Heilman took out the first patent for an embroidery machine, whose special feature was that it operated 200 needles simultaneously. Today's machines operate over 1,000 needles.

Corsetière

In the 19th century, there was great debate about the merits or otherwise of corsets. The Rational Dress Society declared that they were unnatural, but women who did not wear them were considered immoral, loose in more ways than one. It was clear that extremes of tight lacing were a danger to health. Today, in an age of jeans and T-shirts, few women wear them – but they occasionally appear on the catwalk. The profession of corsetière still exists, but today's woman will probably only wear a 'boned' dress for a few hours at a party, not for the entire day.

2 The embroiderer uses a pounce of black chalk to transfer the design through the perforations onto the material to be embroidered.

3 The beads are placed one at a time along the black chalk tracing and embroidered into position.

1 When the design is ready, it is reproduced on perforated tracing paper.

Machine-made lace can vary from the simple to the very elaborate and is used in both haute couture and prêt-à-porter, as well as for lingerie. Much of this lace is produced on Leavers machines, named after John Leavers, who in 1813 developed a method of mechanically twisting together threads to form a fast net. A Jacquard loom is responsible for producing the various patterns. Leavers machines are now used all over the world for lace production and can reproduce the famous classic types of lace – Valenciennes, Brussels, Alençon etc. – or create completely new motifs. When it comes to haute couture lace, the size of the machines places certain constraints on the design. It cannot be bigger than 20 cm, and can only be reproduced in a single run in lengths of 4 m and widths of 90 cm. Following the machine process, basic ecru (unbleached) lace then has to be boiled, bleached and dyed, before being finished and machine-edged.

Fashion industry skills: millinery and working with artificial flowers and feathers

Milliner

This is a profession that stretches back into the mists of time. Hats may not be so popular today as they were fifty years ago, but the wild creations of artist-designers like Marie Mercié, Philippe Model, Jacques le Corre, Steven Jones and Philip Treacy have caused something of a revival. Making a hat involves a series of long processes. Once the sketch has been approved, a prototype is made in *sparterie*. Many people don't realise that there is a distinction between hatters and milliners. The hatter forms the hat, stiffens it with starch, steams it, and shapes it on a lime-wood mould, before drying it in a metal cabinet. The milliner deals with assembly and trimming, and also sews hats. This is a profession that demands a high degree of skill, combined with meticulous attention to detail.

Plumassier

The word plumassier is used for a person working with feathers, and the profession still exists in France. The plumassier's workshop is a riot of exotic colours, like a Noah's Ark reserved entirely for birds. The ostrich feathers are turquoise, the hen's fuchsia, the cock's speckled with saffron... Plumassiers make accessories from bird's feathers for haute couture and for hats as well as for the theatre and cabaret. This profession calls for a good sense of colour, dexterity, taste, and meticulous accuracy, because feathers are fragile. As rare species are protected, only ostrich feathers and those from domestic birds may now be used. The feathers have to be cleaned and dyed, then shaped and cut, before being sewn onto the garment or hat.

Crumpled between her agile fingers, cotton fabric is transformed into camellias and roses will never fade. The creations of the artificial flower maker are only just eclipsed by the real thing.

Artificial flower makers conjure petals, flower spikes, pistils, stamens, buds and leaves from materials varying from cotton to silk, or even plastic or paper. They are also called on to create mock fruit and vegetables that imitate nature as closely as possible. The role of the artificial flower maker is similar to that of the plumassier – their skills are not only required by the fashion industry, but also by show business and anywhere else everlasting flowers might be needed as a decorative feature. There are still specialists working by hand, but most artificial flowers are now made using machines. The fabrics are prepared, cut, dyed, crimped, rolled, glued and mounted. The special tools of the trade – crimping iron, pinking shears, knife etc – have traditionally been handed down from generation to generation over many years.

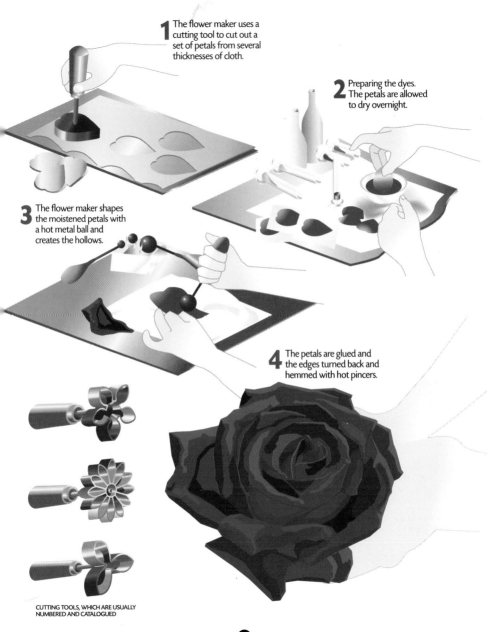

1 The flower maker uses a cutting tool to cut out a set of petals from several thicknesses of cloth.

2 Preparing the dyes. The petals are allowed to dry overnight.

3 The flower maker shapes the moistened petals with a hot metal ball and creates the hollows.

4 The petals are glued and the edges turned back and hemmed with hot pincers.

CUTTING TOOLS, WHICH ARE USUALLY NUMBERED AND CATALOGUED

Fashion industry skills:
pleating, braid and button-making

Button-making

Aided by centuries-old tools, which look incongruous amongst the piles of pearls, rubies, mother-of-pearl and horn, the button-maker's art is based on a long tradition. Buttons can be made from every imaginable material: plastic, wood, glass, mother-of-pearl, enamel, strass (paste), pearl, leather, bone, resin – the list is endless. Some of the button-makers' techniques are highly specialist, such as enamelling, working with molten glass, finishing mother-of pearl... They have often had to invent their own tools – a small mallet, pliers, and delicate tweezers – if what they needed to complete the job was not commercially available. Couturiers consider button-makers to be extremely important in the industry, often giving them special commissions, and demanding exclusive rights to use the finished designs.

Braid

Ever since the Italians brought their skills in producing braid to France in the 14th century, this method of adorning fabrics has been highly valued. Braid-makers use a variety of materials in their designs to embellish garments. Their skills in ornamentation are used both by the couture trade and for furnishings. Gold braid, fringes, appliqués or pompoms are created in their workshops, using special tools such as the *échignol*, *laminoir*, *tournette* and *rouet*. Sometimes they are able to provide that final touch to a design that makes all the difference. Braid-making is a profession which requires extremely nimble fingers, knowledge of the history of braid through the centuries, and the ability to interpret and handle hemp, linen, gold and wool, as well as more modern materials, with skill and intelligence. Much of the braid used today in clothing and furnishings is produced industrially.

Pleaters are usually to be found with pencils in their hands drawing strange designs, or 'playing the accordion' with fabrics or cardboard.

Pleating has existed in various forms since the days of the Greek chiton. Couturiers have used a variety of styles – box, flat, nun's, Watteau, Fortuny, sun-ray – in their creations over the years, but the profession is now in danger of dying out. The art of pleating was traditionally handed down from father to son , and demanded not only dexterity, but also an excellent knowledge of mathematics. It is still done by hand for haute couture, using very precise cardboard moulds into which the material to be pleated is placed. After being placed in the mould, the fabric is baked in an oven. Most of the pleating for the prêt-à-porter industry is done entirely by machine.

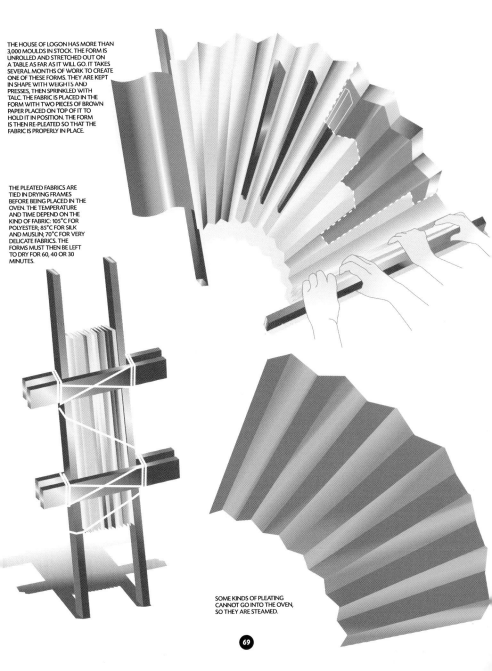

THE HOUSE OF LOGON HAS MORE THAN 3,000 MOULDS IN STOCK. THE FORM IS UNROLLED AND STRETCHED OUT ON A TABLE AS FAR AS IT WILL GO. IT TAKES SEVERAL MONTHS OF WORK TO CREATE ONE OF THESE FORMS. THEY ARE KEPT IN SHAPE WITH WEIGHTS AND PRESSES, THEN SPRINKLED WITH TALC. THE FABRIC IS PLACED IN THE FORM WITH TWO PIECES OF BROWN PAPER PLACED ON TOP OF IT TO HOLD IT IN POSITION. THE FORM IS THEN RE-PLEATED SO THAT THE FABRIC IS PROPERLY IN PLACE.

THE PLEATED FABRICS ARE TIED IN DRYING FRAMES BEFORE BEING PLACED IN THE OVEN. THE TEMPERATURE AND TIME DEPEND ON THE KIND OF FABRIC: 105°C FOR POLYESTER; 85°C FOR SILK AND MUSLIN; 70°C FOR VERY DELICATE FABRICS. THE FORMS MUST THEN BE LEFT TO DRY FOR 60, 40 OR 30 MINUTES.

SOME KINDS OF PLEATING CANNOT GO INTO THE OVEN, SO THEY ARE STEAMED.

Trend consultancies: an increasingly important role

DOMINIQUE PECLERS,
MANAGING DIRECTOR
PECLERS, PARIS

'The relationship between the couturier and the client has been replaced by a system of industrial manufacture that has created a gulf between the product and the client. Today our role consists of organising a successful link with the consumer. We are also called in by companies operating outside the textile sector – cosmetics, cars, computers, telecommunications. Our job is to advise companies seeking added value for their creativity.'

The trend consultancy: where the fashions of tomorrow and the day after are envisioned.

Why do we all fancy having a little black dress or pale muslin curtains at the same time? To ascertain what is happening in fashion, we call on specialists. Always keeping an eye on the new directions of fashion, the trend consultant anticipates the shapes, colours and materials that we will like tomorrow. The consultancy is staffed by people with very different career profiles: artists, graphic designers, sociologists and stylists. They are sensitive to the cultural atmosphere of their time, they leaf through magazines, watch the latest films, comb the fleamarkets, and scan every corner of the horizon in search of new trends. The results of their findings are collected in trend notebooks. This harvest of information enables them to predict the future, and the needs and desires of the next fashion victims. They participate at the design stage as well as the production stage, sensing, analysing, speculating, advising, imagining and communicating. Globalisation has meant that the profession can now adapt its advice to suit companies throughout the world, manufacturing all kinds of products, not just within the fashion industry.

SEBASTIEN DE DIESBACH,
MANAGING DIRECTOR
OF PROMOSTYL

'Knowing how to present cultures which break all the canons of good taste and drawing inspiration from marginal civilisations are imperatives for the profession. The prospects are good for the creative professions, because our society is fashion-oriented. With the globalisation of communications (notably the Web) and uniformity of tastes, you are bound to be caught up in the changes. You have to call on the services of design and fashion in order to attract attention and proclaim your individuality.'

sans formalités
informal

techniques allégés
lightened synthetics

70

Grand couturier:
the garment takes shape

Because couturiers have generally spent several years training with more experienced designers, they feel the urge to create rather than simply produce. They aim to provide unique outfits for a discerning clientele. Entirely hand-made, the garments are very expensive, but the cost is justified by the sheer number of hours' work that goes into making each one. Couturiers are surrounded by a large team of designers, (workshop manager and deputy, seamstress, hand-finishers...), and the team will also include a director of haute couture, an artistic director and an assistant. The couturier's role is to design the collections, the prototypes of which will be shown to the press during the spring-summer and autumn-winter shows. The craftspeople who work with the couturier create exclusive fabrics, embroideries and accessories for each garment. Aspiring couturiers frequently obtain their fashion training at colleges, which often offer work placements within the industry, from small designers to multinational companies, as part of the courses. To earn the name of grand couturier in Paris you must fulfil the criteria imposed by the Chambre Syndicale de la Haute Couture et du Prêt-à-Porter. You must employ at least 20 people in your own workshop; show a collection of at least 75 designs using three live models in Paris twice a year; and finally you must present the collection 45 times a year to customers.

Créateur

The term créateur, as opposed to couturier was first used in Paris to describe a fashion designer about 30 years ago, when Didier Grumbach founded the company Créateurs et Industriels. Halfway between haute couture and prêt-à-porter, the concept of créateur gave a new status to designers who could henceforth label their models with their own name and achieve fame. In 1973, the Fondation Française de la Couture et du Prêt-à-Porter recognised the existence of créateurs and accepted them into the foundation. Thanks to this initiative, young designers in France can now show their clothes without having achieved the status of couturier.

JEAN-CHARLES DE CASTELBAJAC SEES THESE GIRLS IN TARTAN.

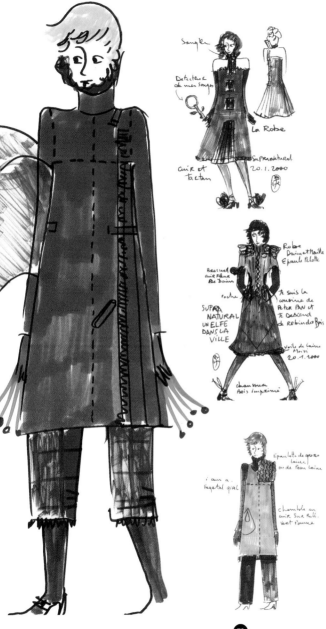

The concept of a designer within prêt-à-porter first appeared in the 1960s. It was recognised that the fashion industry needed people to define the themes and dream up the look for a collection. These designers select the materials, design the models and also need to have a knowledge of marketing. After each collection, they study the results and adjust or update certain models accordingly. They also need to be sensitive to trends, and observe what is being created around them. In close collaboration with the team working on a collection, they supervise the finishing of the models and make sure that the prototypes have the desired cut. They must combine creativity with business sense, and the smaller the business, the more involved they will become with the day-to-day running of it. In recent years, many larger retail companies have cut back the number of designers working for them, relying on suppliers to carry out design work.

Textile designer and engineer: choosing materials and inventing colourways

If the fashion world wants to come up with something new, it gambles on materials, looks, colours and textures. Textile designers have a key role in this process, creating new fabrics appropriate to the seasons, when required by the professional salons and in agreement with the trend consultants. Whether they are working in fashion, furnishings, or interior decoration, textile designers are experts, specialising in printing, knitting or weaving. Twice a year, they define their range of colours, choice of fibres and materials on which to print. Professional illustrators may be employed to translate their ideas onto the fabrics.

Collaboration with the textile engineer

Textile designers' skills are based on their knowledge of the physical and chemical properties of the fibres they work with and the fibres' reaction to various dyes. They also need to be able to adapt their creative ideas to the technical constraints of industrial manufacture and may be in charge of the entire production process for a fabric. The invention of new fibres has brought scientists into the front rank. Textile designers are at the creative end of the process, often calling on textile engineers to carry out more specialised research in the laboratory. The two professions are closely linked. Textile engineers invent new fibres, which the designers can then test in made-up garments. An applied arts training allows textile designers to develop a creative spirit, which also has to be complemented by more technical training. There are colleges offering courses in textile arts and degrees in decorative arts. Textile engineers are expected to take science A levels, followed by a degree. Both routes can open the doors to jobs in the design and packaging sector of the industry.

The mechanics of fabric printing

This process is similar to the technique of silk-screen printing. The textile designer creates the pattern on paper, before printing it on the fabric. Then a frame is created for each print, making it possible to reproduce the pattern over the whole length of the cloth. The fabric is printed using enormous rotating stencils, which can print up to 40,000 m of fabric at a time.

Pattern cutting and the role of the garment technologist

The garment technologist bridges the gap between design and production of the garment.

Garment technologists have the all-important job of planning the way in which a garment will be made. They decide, for example, what thread to use, the seam and stitch types, and the sorts of machinery that will produce the garment. Finally, and most importantly, they assess the costs that will be involved at each stage of manufacture. If it seems that the costs will be prohibitive, the garment technologist will liaise with the designer in the hope of achieving a compromise. Once agreement has been reached, the pieces of fabric are cut out and handed over to a sample machinist, who uses a sewing machine to assemble the pieces to form the garment. The prototype is then ready. A grader then adapts the pattern to different sizes. The final stages of the job are trying the pattern out on the Stockman tailor's dummy and adjusting it. By seeing the way the garment hangs on the dummy the technologist can tell what, if any, changes need to be made.

Pattern-cutting

The pattern is produced on card and the different parts of a garment (back, front, collar, and also lining, pockets, reinforcements...) cut out so that the garment can be put into mass production. This is known as flat cutting. Computers are used to position the different parts of the garment on the piece of fabric to achieve the minimum of wastage.

Modelling the garment on a dressmaker's dummy

Once a design has been agreed, the pattern is produced three-dimensionally on a *Stockman* by placing the *toile* directly onto the dummy, using pins to create the folds and gathers. The designer marks up the reference points on the toile which is then placed onto cardboard in order to produce a prototype pattern, from which the various parts of the garment can be cut out.

THE *MODÉLISTE* (DRESS DESIGNER) PLACES THE TOILE DIRECTLY ONTO THE STOCKMAN, OR DUMM[...]

Pattern Making (100%

THE ROLE OF THE COMPUTER

Lay planners work out how to cut out the pieces of fabric in the most economical way, and the computer is now an invaluable tool in this process. Computer-aided design and manufacture make it possible to obtain satisfactory results quickly for a large number of other operations within the industry.

THE PATTERN-CUTTER
REPRODUCES THE
PATTERN IN COTTON
ON CARDBOARD.

Grader and bulk cutter: mass produced models

THE PATTERN IS TACKED ONTO THE FABRIC.

THE OUTLINE IS TRACED ONTO THE FABRIC WITH CHALK.

ALL THAT REMAINS IS TO CUT ROUND THE OUTLINE.

Bulk cutter

Using special machines, the fabric is unrolled onto a cutting table and folded over on itself several times to form a 'mattress'. In this way, several pieces of fabric can be cut at one time. Even though the whole operation can now be controlled by computers, many cutters prefer to use their hands to guide the mobile cutters or band saws themselves. Accurate movements are essential, as the slightest error could affect the entire manufacturing process.

Pattern grader

Starting from a standard size pattern, the grader adapts it for all the sizes that will be commercially produced. Software produced by companies such as Lectra or VetiGraph that is based on European standards are used to make the necessary calculations.

22.7

14.6

EUROPEAN UNION

HONG KONG

From fibre to fabric

The textile industry transforms fibre into fabric in four stages.

Spinning
Spinning can be defined as the series of operations by which the raw material is turned into yarn. The techniques employed vary according to the nature of the fibre (animal, vegetable or artificial).

Weaving
Weaving consists of interlacing the warp (lengthways) yarn and the weft (widthways) yarn. The weave determines the way the yarns are interlaced. The most common weaves are plain, twill and satin, and all others are variations on these. Plain is the simplest, the threads going under and over, the warp and weft crossing just once each time. Twill involves the weft and warp crossing each other more than once before going under, and gives a diagonal effect Satin involves even more crossovers than twill, and results in a smooth, unbroken, shiny finish.

Knitting
Unlike weaving, knitting forms stitches using only a single yarn. New stitches are tried out on a hand-operated machine, before being employed on an industrial scale on tubular knitting machines.

Finishing
It is during this final stage that the fabric gets its finished look. It will be bleached, dyed, printed and/or sized. Sizing has two possible functions. Firstly it can be used to alter the feel of a fabric, giving it strength or weight. Traditionally, gum or starch has been used for this, but because this tends to wash out eventually, new technological processes are now being employed. Sizing can also mean using chemicals to add a protective quality to fabric, making it flameproof, waterproof, antibacterial etc.

MAJOR TEXTILE EXPORTERS IN 1999 (IN BILLIONS OF DOLLARS)

CHINA	SOUTH KOREA	TAIWAN	UNITED STATES	JAPAN	INDIA	PAKISTAN	TURKEY
13.8	13.3	12.7	9.2	6.8	5	4.6	3.3

Production managers and machinists: industrial manufacture

Production managers are responsible for a production unit and oversee all the stages in the creation of a garment.

After the technical specifications for a garment have been agreed (model, colourways, materials, quantities, time available for completion), production managers supervise the manufacture of the range. They assess the production time, inform the factories about the technical requirements and are responsible for quality control. They work out and manage the production flow systems, ensuring that each element in the process of manufacturing will run smoothly, without bottlenecks. The job demands good technical understanding, precision and accuracy.

THE FIRST PROTOTYPE LEAVES THE DESIGNER'S STUDIO. IT WILL LATER BE MADE UP IN THE FACTORY.

Sample machinist

Sample machinists make up the prototypes of the garments. As they put the different parts of the garment together, they can point out any manufacturing problems that are likely to occur and make sure that everything is correctly positioned – the pockets, zips, Velcro etc. – and adjust seam widths and darts as necessary. Any relevant comments from the sample machinist are passed on to the production manager, the garment technologist and the design team, who will then start production. With supplementary training, sample machinists can specialise in a particular material or discipline, such as embroidery, leather or fur.

Machinist

European clothing workshops work mainly on short runs; the big production runs producing thousands of copies of a garment tend to take place further afield in countries where labour is cheaper. In the past, machinists would have specialised in a single operation, but nowadays they are expected to master all stages of assembly and to be able to use several machines – ordinary sewing machines, overlockers, embroidery machines, buttonholers, etc. The machinists begin by sewing straight seams on flat-bed machines, before moving on to working with stretch fabrics like jersey on specialist machines.

THE FABRIC PASSES THROUGH AT A CONSTANT SPEED.

THE MACHINIST PUTS THE MAIN PIECES TOGETHER.

THEN SHE DOES THE FINISHING.

Buyer, product manager and sourcing: the company image

In the 1980s, increasingly fierce competition resulted in the creation of the position of product manager, whose job it is to oversee a product from design to marketing. The job involves analysing the market, assessing a product's position within the market (which particular group of consumers is the product aimed at?), and ensuring that it is suitable for the target area before setting up a marketing strategy. Product managers try to predict the target consumers' needs and adapt the product to the market. Their duties combine a creative process (informing the designers of current trends, planning the collections or developing brands) with logistics (checking the production process, quality and marketing). Product managers must have complementary qualities – powers of analysis, and organisational ability on the one hand, and intuition and sensitivity to market movements on the other. Training in commerce, marketing and management are the basic requirements, and specialisation in fashion management is an added advantage.

Buyer

The role of the buyer varies from company to company. Some have influence over design, but for others the job will involve choosing designs already in production. Some buyers in prêt-à-porter take charge of selecting materials, control deliveries and stock control and deal with the range as a whole. To obtain a product which will make an impression on the market and sell well, buyers analyse recent sales and speculate about future sales. They check out suppliers to ensure that they are getting the best value for money. In some sectors like mass distribution, their job overlaps that of product manager. Buyers are able to influence and have a say in various parts of the business – style, quality, marketing, logistics and technology. They must combine management and negotiating abilities.

Sourcing

Sourcing is becoming increasingly important in the industry and is defined as finding suppliers abroad who will be able to provide finished products or raw materials with which to make the products. The sourcers' role may be limited to seeking out raw materials, which requires the talents of a buyer and a grounding in marketing, but they may also extend their field of activity to organising production of a garment at an overseas factory. For this, companies recruit engineers or highly competent textile technicians capable of supervising the manufacturing process. Sourcing can be dictated by economics – if it simply becomes too expensive to produce a garment at home, it will have to be sourced abroad.

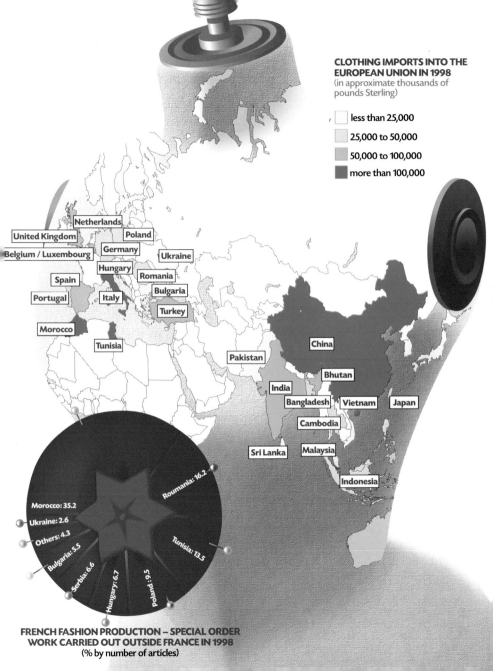

CLOTHING IMPORTS INTO THE EUROPEAN UNION IN 1998
(in approximate thousands of pounds Sterling)

less than 25,000

25,000 to 50,000

50,000 to 100,000

more than 100,000

Netherlands

United Kingdom

Belgium / Luxembourg

Poland

Germany

Ukraine

Hungary

Spain

Romania

Portugal

Italy

Bulgaria

Turkey

Morocco

Tunisia

China

Pakistan

Bhutan

India

Bangladesh

Vietnam

Japan

Cambodia

Sri Lanka

Malaysia

Indonesia

Roumania: 16.2

Morocco: 35.2

Ukraine: 2.6

Others: 4.3

Tunisia: 13.5

Bulgaria: 5.5

Serbia: 6.6

Hungary: 6.7

Poland: 9.5

**FRENCH FASHION PRODUCTION – SPECIAL ORDER
WORK CARRIED OUT OUTSIDE FRANCE IN 1998**
(% by number of articles)

Merchandiser, salesperson and shop assistant: the importance of these roles

In the very competitive world of the fashion industry where there are so many companies and designers vying for a share of the market, merchandising has become an absolute necessity. The use of brand names and logos, and establishing the names of the designers are strategies involved in creating the all-important visual identity. The role of the merchandiser includes managing the display space, lighting, choice of materials and furnishings. It has recently become common practice to add an attraction such as a small café, a florist or a magazine counter to a sales area in a bid to give the customer an added reason to visit and browse.

Salesperson

Salespeople sell their company's products to the buyers of other companies, so they must enjoy contact with people, have good powers of persuasion and a head for figures. They need a thorough knowledge of their product (including manufacturing techniques and quality of materials) so that they can answer any questions about it and promote it. They also have to be able to convince the buyer of the merits of their product and negotiate the price to clinch a deal. The salesperson also needs to discuss methods of payment and oversee the smooth running of operations – delivery, invoicing – and generally ensure customer satisfaction. Finally, salespeople also need to be aware of the position of their product in the market and always be on the lookout for new contracts.

Personality is all-important for a salesperson. This job demands good social skills, and the ability to listen and argue convincingly. Dynamism, assurance and efficiency are also essential. The ideal career profile is a degree from a business school.

Shop assistant

Shop assistants are in direct contact with the general public, and are the final link in the chain. Their function, which is similar to that of the salesperson, is to encourage people to buy. They need to be able to advise on size or colour and sense when a customer prefers to be left to browse alone, or requires some personal attention. Shop assistants are also responsible for maintaining the company image, so a smart appearance is important. Selling is open to people with many different career profiles, and it is always possible for people without formal qualifications to show that they have the personal qualities that will make all the difference.

Model, make-up artist, hairdresser and photographer: all helping to promote the clothes

Beautiful, tall, slim, and sophisticated, catwalk models make the designers' clothes look sensational and the customers believe that if they buy that dress, a little of the glamour just might rub off on them.

The successful model today is a formidable businesswoman, often deciding which brand she will represent and which photographer's lens she prefers to be captured by. Model agencies are very powerful too, with Draconian selection criteria and strictly negotiating their models' hours of work.

Hairdresser

Surely the woman and the model's best friend, the hairdresser tries their utmost to find innovative ways to stretch, relax, pull, brush, curl, dye, cut, hide or twist hair, moulding it according to the latest trends. Hairstylists create different cuts twice a year for shows that are reserved for professionals in the industry. Studio hairdressers have a different role from those who work in salons. Their styles are ephemeral, being created for a single show or photo session. The art of hairdressing requires dexterity and a sense of harmony and proportion.

Photographer

The critic Susan Sontag once wrote: 'The greatest fashion photography is more than the photography of fashion.' Fashion photography today is not simply a reflection of the subject matter, but seeks to comment on it, which explains why some of the world's greatest photographers have chosen to work in this area. A series of exciting fashion photographs that catch the eye and spur the imagination will play a large part in selling clothes. Many photographers begin work for agencies or newspapers and magazines, eventually branching out to work freelance and run their own studios.

Make-up artist

Make-up artists have an infallible eye for the unsightly blemish. They will not let a red patch or a spot escape them, and with their cunning blends of cosmetics they can shade an eyelid, round out a mouth or blur the outline of a chin. Make-up artists must keep a close eye on trends as they work with ever-changing product lines that are created twice a year, summer and winter, by the many cosmetic manufacturers. 'A good make-up artist is first and foremost a good psychologist,' says Viktoria Pjebyska, who has stopped counting how many haute couture shows and fashion shoots for magazines she has done. 'You need a lot of creativity, sensitivity, and to follow the golden rule: everything must be in harmony, whether the make-up is pale or more substantial.'

The importance of press and public relations

The clothes have been designed, made and shown on the catwalk. Now they have to be sold. That is where the media come in, summoned by the press officer.

Press officers are the link between the product (the brand, the designer) and the journalist. They present information about the clothes in a press file. This summarises a show, and traces the history of a garment or advertises the launch of a new product. Press officers also organise events, send out invitation cards, plan interviews and lend out the clothes for photo sessions – the intention being to gain the maximum amount of press coverage. Public relations consultants are playing an increased role in the fashion industry, helping to market clothes through organising events, advertising and other forms of publicity. To be suited for these roles you need to be good at and enjoy communicating with people both verbally and in writing.

Fashion stylist

Stylists are experts in presenting clothes to achieve the maximum effect. They are responsible for choosing the hairstyles, make-up and accessories that will enhance the appearance of the garments on the model. It is an increasingly crucial role within the fashion industry, as new collections have to achieve an immediate impact on the catwalk or through photographs.

Fashion journalism

Fashion editors are usually attached to newspapers in which they have a regular column. The success or failure of a garment may sometimes depend on whether or not the fashion editor decides to praise it. Following a given theme, fashion correspondents go through the shops collecting clothes and accessories which will appear on the fashion pages of magazines. They work together with stylists to achieve the right look. Many correspondents work freelance.

SHORE THING: coastal vote. *This page, above,* 'Stretch' cafe table, POA, by Schamburg and Alvisse. *On table, from left,* glass vase, AUS$950, by Mona Schildt for Kosta from Form Follows Function. **Table lamp,** AUS$650, from Chee Soon & Fitzgerald. 'Mariage Frères' tea-scented candle, AUS$85, from La Lavande. 50s cricket-ball cigarette dispenser, AUS$15, from the Rocks Market, Sydney. *Left,* 'Whistle' chairs, AUS$885 each, by Norman & Quaine. Hand-painted silk cushions, AUS$120, by David Cheah from Chee Soon & Fitzgerald. 'Stretch' cafe table, as above. 'Stretch' stool, AUS$350, by Schamburg & Alvisse. *On stool,* 'Holmegaard' glass bowl, AUS$450, from Chee Soon & Fitzgerald. **Wool rug,** AUS$2,300, from Chee Soon & Fitzgerald. 'Curly Swirl' mounted wallpaper, AUS$180 per 50m roll, by Florence Broadhurst from Chee Soon & Fitzgerald. *Opposite page,* she wears printed cotton blouse by Magnus Flobecker. Silver necklace, SEK7,900, by Georg Jensen. 'Curly Swirl' wallpaper, as before

towels and lush specimen palm plants. For maximum flexibility, nine-foot-high floors of windowless, vented empty space (devoted solely to pipes and ducts) are layered between the levels devoted to research. Outdoor corridors enwrap the vast glass-walled laboratories, where empty cages still smell sweet with the musk of lab rats lost in the institute's holy war on disease. Even the treads of the 24 principal stairways are travertine, the expensive Italian marble pitted with shallow holes that match the bubbles in Kahn's silky cast-concrete walls.

The institute's operating costs are high, and despite the continued presence of three Nobel laureates, tight funding means the management has begun sponsoring sunset symphonies in the courtyard to coax small change from La Jolla's elite. A takeaway brochure for the elderly details the tax advantages of donating their houses to science.

Salk's original faculty of thirteen senior scientists has quadrupled. More than 700 workers now crowd on to the site each day, and expansion has been inevitable. Although there is more to the original institute scheme than Dr Salk built, Kahn's Salk Meeting House remains on the drawing board, and the nearest it has come to reality is a photo-realistic digital model by architect Kent Larson (ironically, some $22 million was spent on a 1995 expansion that clutters the composition without enhancing it). Today, suburbia crowds the southern edge of the site, where, it is rumoured,

Create your own designer bag

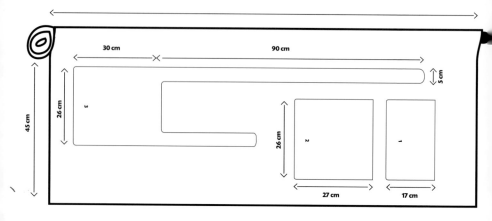

1 CUTTING PLAN
Cut three pieces of fabric with the measurements shown above.

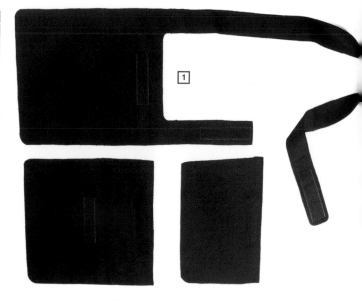

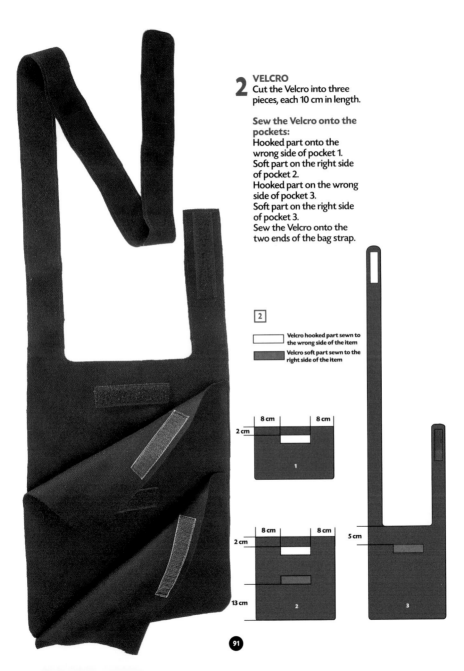

2 VELCRO

Cut the Velcro into three pieces, each 10 cm in length.

Sew the Velcro onto the pockets:
Hooked part onto the wrong side of pocket 1.
Soft part on the right side of pocket 2.
Hooked part on the wrong side of pocket 3.
Soft part on the right side of pocket 3.
Sew the Velcro onto the two ends of the bag strap.

2

☐ Velcro hooked part sewn to the wrong side of the item

▨ Velcro soft part sewn to the right side of the item

8 cm | 8 cm
2 cm

1

8 cm | 8 cm
2 cm

13 cm | 2

5 cm

3

FROM A PROTOTYPE BY
ANNE BOYÉ

BARÔUE ROUGE

3

3 MAKING UP
Place the three
pieces one on
top of the
other and sew
them together.

FIND OUT

WHAT IS INTELLIGENT CLOTHING? ARTIFICIAL OR SYNTHETIC?
DESIGN CLASSICS OF THE 20TH CENTURY.
BRITISH BUYING HABITS.
USEFUL ADDRESSES TO FIND OUT MORE.

Intelligent clothes

The textile sector today is now a high-tech industry, aiming to combine comfort, hygiene and safety.

Clothing: a functional as well as attractive product

The new fibres match the needs of today's consumers. Urban living, central heating, air conditioning, public transport all demand a new order of textile components, and favour the rise of biotextiles. Clothing is no longer simply ruled by the dictates of fashion and is a very functional, even multifunctional, product. Technofibres are developed through new technology, incorporating computer-aided design techniques, and usually involve a combination of traditional fibres with newly created substances, providing new aesthetics and/or protective, hard-wearing qualities.

Combatting nasty smells ...

Once reserved for the medical corps, antibacterial fabrics took over the world of sport before coming into general use. The antibacterial function, their ability to combat nasty smells, was the first to attract the attention of researchers. Sportsmen and women now benefit from ever more sophisticated textiles. When the first experiments were carried out, the antibacterial agents were added during the finishing process. Today, in order to be more effective, they are integrated into the very heart of the fibre, welded to it by ultra-resistant chemicals. This process consists of introducing mini-capsules, which diffuse their antibacterial properties over the fibres during spinning. Encouraged by this discovery, scientists have extended the principle to give fabrics other properties, such as anti-

mosquito, anti-UV rays (fibres being charged with metallic oxides), anti-marking (treated with Teflon), anti-stress, anti-tobacco etc. Like cosmetics, certain fabrics are also moisturising, slimming or perfumed.

A garment in harmony with nature

In response to the popularity of outdoor activities, where contact with nature may be brutal, researchers have perfected very resistant textiles. To the demand for protection and reliability may be added the criteria of flexibility, lightness and comfort. So polyamide fibres, among them Cordura, made by Du Pont, are combined with particles of stainless steel or quartz, which guarantee the strength of the products. Because they are lightweight and waterproof, these products are already a major influence in sportswear. Ceramic yarns have been introduced into swimwear, because it is claimed that they help prevent body temperature dropping suddenly when a swimmer gets out of the water.

Fibres which adapt to the seasons

Studies are under way to improve what was originally the main aim of clothing – that is to protect us from variations in climate. Unitika have developed a type of yarn based on a ceramic core that can capture solar energy and convert it into heat. a very useful feature in polar regions. Sympatex, developed in Germany, allows perspiration molecules to pass through, but no water can penetrate the other way. It is dense, so that the wearer will not feel the cold in high winds, but the membrane will remain breathable for a long time. Gore-Tex, originally developed for space travel, uses a membrane made from a substance similar to Teflon, and is rainproof, windproof and breathable.

Garment for a blind person.
Concept: Gilles Vittbeck and Rémi Ozello-Brocco.
Fashion: William Leon.

21st century clothes

Sportswear also makes use of the new fibres for their reflective properties, which can radiate over 150 metres. Street wear has adopted the material used in road signs and the safety factor has become a new fashion phenomenon, with urban street signs and other pictograms on a Scotchlite backing. Thermochromic textiles which change colour according to the temperature will someday probably be able to tell us the dose of UV rays we have received, the degree of pollution or the proportion of allergens present in the atmosphere. Soon each component in our wardrobe will have a function – the medical T-shirt that keeps you informed about your health, shoes equipped with a GPS (global positioning system) to keep you on the right track, glasses linked to the Internet, or computer chips integrated into the fabric...

From artificial to synthetic

Chemical fibres can be split into two families: artificial fibres, based on vegetable cellulose (acetate and viscose), and synthetic fibres, based on products derived from petroleum (polyamide or nylon, polyester, acrylic).

Artificial fibres

These are made from modified vegetable or animal fibres. After six years' research, Hilaire Bernigaud de Chardonnet (1839–1924) of the École Polytechnique in Paris experimented with the first manufacturing process for artificial silk, using mulberry leaves. Artificial silk was launched at the time of the Paris *Exposition Universelle* of 1899, but was rapidly replaced by viscose and acetate made from cellulose. Light, fluid and crease-resistant, this new fibre was widely used in lingerie before it was supplanted by synthetics. Artificial fibres today incorporate antibacterial molecules and have regained their place at centre stage.

Synthetic fibres

Nylon is 'as strong as steel, as fine as the threads of a spider's web, and has a splendid sheen!' according to an advertisement. In 1935, Du Pont invented the first fibre to be entirely manufactured from carbon, hydrogen, nitrogen and oxygen. Nylon, or polyamide 6.6, was first used for toothbrushes, but really took off when it was used to produce stockings. In 1939, the year they went on the market, 64 million pairs of nylons were sold in the United States. During the Second World War, nylon production was devoted to the making of parachutes and other items necessary for the war effort, but once the war was over the nylon stocking became a raging success with women all over the world. When they were

asked what they had missed most during the war, 33 per cent of American women said men, and 67 per cent nylons. (Source: Du Pont).

Lycra

Also created by Du Pont, in 1959, this filament with a three to ten per cent elastane base is even stronger, more elastic and more comfortable than nylon. Originally used in corsetry, Lycra has revolutionised sportswear, lingerie and particularly swimsuits. In the modern age of stretch fabrics, Lycra is widely used. During the 1980s, the nylon-Lycra combination used in tights and stockings made a spectacular breakthrough and opened the way to unequalled comfort and durability.

Synthetic paper

Du Pont continues to experiment with new substances, and in 1995–96 Hussein Chalayan presented designs made from synthetic paper developed by the company called Tyvek, which was developed for protective clothing.

Microfibres

The first polyester-based microfibres which appeared during the 1980s were breathable (they allow the skin to breathe through the material) and wind-resistant (thanks to their very closely woven texture). Although they were first used in sportswear, they now form a part of everyday street clothing.

Blending: the secret of the fibres of the future

Today natural and chemical fibres are mixed to reduce production costs, develop different textures, subtler colours, and above all to avoid exhausting the planet's resources.

Natural fibres

These are obtained from animals such as sheep (wool), goats (mohair, cashmere), llama (angora), silkworm (silk), or from plants such as cotton, flax, hemp, jute and natural rubber. In order to compete with synthetic fibres, the professional associations for natural fibres set up labels denoting a standard for quality, like the Woolmark for wool (1964) or Pure Cotton for cotton (1968). Natural fibres are comfortable, absorbent and breathable, while artificial fibres are easy-care, cheap and strong. By mixing the two, the advantages of both can be combined. Due to the number of new fibres that have been developed, since 1963 manufacturers have been obliged to state the composition of fibres in a garment on the label.

Synthetic or natural?

Since the green movement began, we have become accustomed to questions about the protection of the planet. Nowadays the old 'synthetic versus natural' debate has been replaced by the more worrying question of the pollution resulting from the manufacture of the product. It is important to note that the production of natural fibres sometimes causes more pollution than that of artificial fibres. For instance, dyeing cotton calls for the use of large amounts of water, which become polluted as a result. One way to combat the worries of pollution is recycling. Rhovil-Eco is a synthetic fibre made from recycled PVC mineral water bottles. 20 one-and-a-half-litre bottles give enough yarn to knit a child's jumper. In 1992, Paco Rabanne created an ecological tunic made from a collection of plastic water bottles.

The clothes and accessories of the 20th century

Jeans

Jean was originally a cotton fabric for sailors' trousers, made in Genoa in 1567. The comfortable, strong, cheap material used by Levi Strauss in 1853 for the first pair of what were to become his world famous trousers came from Nîmes in France and was christened 'denim', or de Nîmes, 'from Nîmes' in French. Strauss, who had emigrated from Bavaria, started making these hard-wearing trousers for the miners and gold prospectors of the American West. Europe discovered the trousers at the end of the Second World War. Popularised by American stars such as James Dean, Elvis Presley and Marilyn Monroe, jeans became a huge success with everyone, from teenagers to workmen and rock stars. A pair of worn, faded flared Levis became the symbol of the 1960s and the student generation. Levis Jeans are characterised by their five pockets, buttoned flies, copper rivets, orange topstitching, imitation leather label at the rear and the famous red-orange 'tab'.

The T-shirt

Originally a male undergarment, the T-shirt appeared in 1899 in the ranks of the American navy. By 1920 it was being worn by UCLA students when indulging in sporting activities. Inspired by the T shape, the US Navy christened it the *T type shirt* in 1942. In 1957 it became an entirely different garment, worn by both men and women. A simple design, when printed, it became a way of making a statement, proclaiming anything from 'I love New York' to 'Surfers do it standing up', as well as being an ideal medium for advertising.

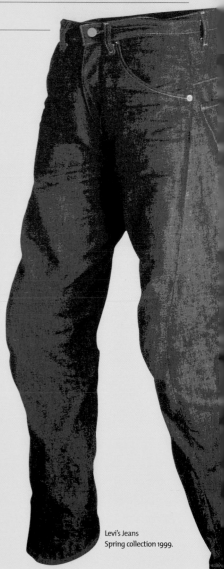

Levi's Jeans
Spring collection 1999.

The bra

No one is quite sure who created the bra, but the first patent was taken out in 1914 by Mary Phelps Jacob in the United States. Her design consisted of two handkerchiefs sewn together with ribbons, and she naively sold the patent to the Warner company for just $1500. Until the mid-1920s, the bra was used to flatten the bust and push it downwards, in keeping with the androgynous look favoured by young women of the time. With changes in fashion, the corsetry companies began to manufacture bras boned and stitched into different cup sizes. In the 1940s, pads were incorporated to give additional shape, and in the 1950s, the outline became the most exaggerated ever, with conical cups. The bra continues to develop, with attempts to reconcile the requirements of beauty and comfort.

Nylons

Nylon stockings replaced those made from artificial silk that had been produced since the end of the 19th century, and were cheaper and more durable. In the immediate post-war years, supply could not keep up with demand, and many women had to resort to the black market to obtain them. Seamless stockings were introduced in the 1950s, and now seams are only incorporated for decorative effect. At various times, depending on skirt length, highly patterned stockings have been in vogue. The arrival of the miniskirt and the development of tights in the 1960s seemed to spell the end of stockings, but longer skirt lengths in the 1970s and 1980s saw a resurgence in their popularity. Improvements in hold-up designs, obviating the need for suspenders, and the

An assortment of women's bras. Mizz Magazine, October 2000

attraction of stockings for erotic or health reasons seem likely to mean they will continue to have a market.

The little black dress

'Dress a woman in black or white at a party. She will be the one most looked at,' said Coco Chanel in the year she created her simple long-sleeved crepe de Chine sheath dress. It was immediately christened 'the Ford signed by Chanel' in the November 1926 edition of *Vogue*. From then on all the couturiers would have a little black dress in their collections. Molyneux joined Chanel in promoting it during the 1930s, and during the war, Balenciaga created one which could be transformed by adding a flounce, enabling you to change your day dress into evening wear, a very practical idea in this time of austerity.

1937: the Perfecto

This thick leather blouson, the only thing to wear with jeans, is characterised by numerous zips and a collar fastened with press studs. Although invented before the Second World War, it really took off in the 1950s when Harley Davidson subcontracted the famous leathers for motorcycle wear. The jacket became world famous through the film *The Wild One* (1954). A relative of the leather motorcycle jacket is the bomber jacket, designed by Irving Schott for use by the US air force, hence the name.

1946: The bikini

In July 1946, a few days after the first nuclear test on Bikini Atoll, the French industrialist Louis Réard launched his own bomb during a 'water party' at the Molitor swimming pool. It was a new two-piece swimsuit, kept in place by strings, and its name was to become part of everyday language. It was so small that only Michèle Bernardini, star dancer at the Casino de Paris, dared model it... Parisian women adopted it straight away, delighted to be able to show off their tanned bodies on the beaches of the Riviera.

The New Look

Christian Dior's New Look of 1947 took France and the Western World by storm. In a period of postwar economic austerity, he created clothes that were luxurious, extravagant, beautiful and frivolous. The dresses, with their long full skirts, required metres of material, and some Parisian women wearing them were attacked in the streets by impoverished housewives who objected to the flagrant display of wealth. In America, some women objected to Dior's idealising of femininity, and putting women back into corsets, seen as a symbol of male domination. Other women applauded his 'liberation' of female sexuality, and maintained that it was a reflection of their new power in the world. Once again, Paris was established as the centre of Western fashion, and other couturiers had reason to be grateful to Dior. The voluminous skirts and petticoats remained in fashion until near the end of the 1950s, when they were adopted by the rock and roll generation. John Galliano, creative director at Dior, has referred back to the style of the fashion house's founder with his designs of recent years, as Dior himself had drawn inspiration from the styles of his youth.

Jean Cocteau wearing a duffel coat.

1949: The duffel coat

The duffel coat, a three-quarter frog-fastening coat with a hood, cut from thick carded wool fabric, worn by British sailors in the 1940s, was originally manufactured in the town of Duffel in Belgium. Worn by General Montgomery during the Normandy landings, it was made fashionable in France in 1947 by Jean Cocteau, the writer, poet, designer and film director, who was a major customer of the French shop, Old England. In beige, brown or navy blue, it also became the uniform of students, both boys and girls. It has since been reinterpreted by couturiers in softer materials.

1954: The stiletto heel

At the time the great designer Roger Vivier was associated with Christian Dior, he dreamt up witty, extravagant shoes for the couture house which were only available made-to-measure. Vivier regularly invented new heels for them, one style being destined to become a classic – the stiletto, which was designed for both sandals and court shoes. Tapering to a point and seven or eight centimetres high, it made women look taller and gave them a sexy, swaying walk. Glamorous actresses such as Marlene Dietrich, Sophia Loren and Elizabeth Taylor were quick to adopt them, and the style became a huge success all over the world.

1954: The Chanel suit

In 1954, aged 71 and after 15 years of inactivity, Coco Chanel made a very controversial return to the world of fashion. The star of the collection was a delightful little suit, extremely elegant and very light. The special feature of the jacket, which illustrated Chanel's principle that 'the wrong side should be as perfect as the right side', was that it had a lining of the same fabric and the same design as the silk blouse that went with it. The Chanel suit could be worn all day by working women and became a symbol of French good taste. It has been copied again and again all over the world and is a true symbol of the 'total look'.

1965: The miniskirt

Courrèges in Paris or Quant in London? The question of who invented the miniskirt is debatable. Whatever the answer may be, this daring garment appeared in the same year in both countries – white and structured in France, brightly coloured and thigh-length in Great Britain. Much criticised by mothers (who soon took to wearing it themselves), the miniskirt caught on straight away with the girls, and could be found in daytime or evening versions in every fabric imaginable. Right from the start, there was no 'regulation' length in the collections and hems went up and down according to the whims of the couturiers.

Black Gucci stiletto shoe.
Women's Journal, 1997

1965: Tights

In 1958, the French hosiery industry invented a technique that made it possible to knit two stockings at once and join them together. Tights were launched onto the market in 1965, and as soon as they were available they became indispensable, since they provided a modest solution to the problem of suspenders showing below the hemlines of miniskirts. From the late 1960s, nylon stockings, which were less comfortable and stretchy, were widely discarded in favour of tights. Women had to wait until the 1980s for the advent of Lycra. Mixed with Tactel, Lycra is partly responsible for the success of opaque tights, which are now a standard item in women's wardrobes.

1966: The dinner jacket – for women

The year Yves Saint Laurent opened the first Rive Gauche boutique, he put women into dinner jackets – evening garments previously reserved for men, which had first appeared in Monte Carlo at the end of the 19th century. American women wore the tuxedo with ruffled shirts or T-shirts, strolling casually along with their hands in their pockets. This was definitely not the done thing in the world of couture at that time. Since then, every one of Yves Saint Laurent's collections has included a version of his 'lucky' dinner jacket. The late Princess Diana once memorably donned a dinner jacket for an evening engagement.

Punk 'style'

Centred on Vivienne Westwood and Malcolm McLaren's King's Road shop, punk fashion was characterised by deliberate attempts to shock. Hair was shaved in strips, brightly coloured and drawn into glued spikes, faces were painted grotesquely, safety pins were used as earrings and through noses, and clothes were torn, split, and adorned with chains, spikes, studs and other metal objects. T-shirts carried slogans so offensive that sometimes the police were prompted to try and prevent their sale. Although this phenomenon was in some ways regarded as 'anti-fashion', its influence extended to haute couture and ready-to-wear, albeit in a more restrained way.

1970s chic: a textile producer's dream

In the 1970s, everything was wide: wide lapels, kipper ties, flared trousers. Fashion seemed aimed at using as much material as possible. The impression of excess was enhanced by the platform soles and heels that reached their height (literally) in the middle of the decade. Everybody seemed to be wearing those shoes, no matter that they made it almost impossible to walk. But when did fashion ever have to be practical?

Punk lives on – destroy t-shirt and paint splattered jeans.
Mizz Magazine, 2001

Tennis shoes by Bensimon.

The 1980s: The jogging suit

Made up of trousers and a sweatshirt, this casual brushed cotton jersey ensemble, which is both warm and comfortable, was originally a garment for athletes. It started life as a garment for sports training – hence the name jogging suit – and was also known as the tracksuit, but nowadays we need no excuse for wearing it every day. It spread with the 1980s craze for 'working out' intensively. The recent trend for 'wrapping ourselves in cotton wool' has made it our favourite garment for comfort and relaxation, and it started a whole wave of sportswear spilling over into fashion. Sonia Rykiel had a towelling jogging suit in her 1974 autumn-winter collection.

1993: Issey Miyake's Pleats Please

It has often been said that he copied Fortuny, who in turn had been inspired by the ancient world for the cut of his famous Delphos dresses. Issey Miyake's unique fabrics were invented by a fabric technician in Tokyo, and from his first collection in 1973 were an immediate success. He reached his apogee in 1993 with the Pleats Please range. The clothes were crease-resistant, machine-washable, and dried in five minutes. The dresses, trousers, jackets and tunics, were all interchangeable, the cut was inspired by the kimono, and they were available in extraordinary colours. Over the course of the years and the shows, the pieces have been endlessly recombined.

Trainers

The 1930s saw the birth of canvas shoes with rubber soles intended for sport such as plimsolls, tennis shoes, and basketball boots. There have been big changes in sports shoes since the 1970s. All kinds of technical wizardry have been incorporated – injection soles, ventilation systems, anatomical foot supports, fluorescence – trainers can even calculate the runner's speed. Gazelle, Stan Smith, New Balance, Nike, any colour, any shape, trainers today are enjoying the most spectacular success. Sport is invading every fashion outlet from the supermarket to haute couture, and sportswear can be found in nearly everyone's wardrobe, though it's not such a recent phenomenon as one might think – Coco Chanel used to wear white tennis shoes with her jersey suits...

Chuck Taylor All Stars
by Converse.

Word games

He's got it all sewn up:
he has everything how he wants it.

Laughing up one's sleeve:
having a private laugh at someone else's expense.

A blue stocking:
a learned or pedantic woman.

To cut one's coat according to one's cloth:
to make do with what one has or can afford.

Talking through one's hat:
talking nonsense.

To be hand in glove with someone:
to be closely involved in the same (nefarious) busines

He's tied to his mother's apron strings:
he always does what his mother tells him to.

A turncoat:
a traitor.

To take silk:
to become a barrister.

Mad as a hatter:
crazy (many theories exist as to the origin of this saying: according to one, mercury used in the hat-making process affected the workers' mental health).

one's birthday suit: naked.

To have ants in one's pants: to be fidgety.

To have a bee in one's bonnet: to be obsessed with something.

To give someone the boot: to dismiss them from their job.

Don't get your knickers in a twist: don't get angry or upset.

Petticoat government: domination by women.

If the cap fits, wear it: you decide whether this description fits you.

wolf in sheep's clothing: someone dangerous disguised as someone harmless.

Clothing as an art form

Art and fashion have a special link because they are both the result of a creative process. If there is a boundary between fashion and art, it lies in the choice of medium of expression.

Fashion in painting

Industrial fashion creates utilitarian objects, tied to the taste of the times, and therefore ephemeral. Works of art, on the other hand, are made to last and are not attached to a particular function. Artists have often accepted commissions, painting portraits to order. If they were not particularly inspired by their sitters, they would make up for it by concentrating on the details of their costume. This has given us precious information on the history of clothing, hairstyles and jewellery from the delicate ruffs of the Elizabethan age to the dandies of the Georgian era.

Fashion in dance

When Diaghilev, with his taste for modern art, arrived in Paris with the Ballets Russes in 1909, talented artists were for the first time asked to create costumes and scenery for the stage. Goncharova, Bakst, Gris, Benois, Rouault, Picasso and Cocteau among others worked for Diaghilev, and inspired the world of couture. Paul Poiret, who was heavily influenced by Bakst's designs, was the first couturier to come up with the idea of commissioning fabric designs from the painter Raoul Dufy in 1910. And when the young Russian illustrator Romain de Tirtoff, better known as Erté, the French for the initials RT, arrived in Paris in 1912, he too approached Poiret to present his oriental sketches of richly coloured clothes. This was to be the start of a great collaboration, in which they were also joined

by Paul Iribe. Among Paul Poiret's notable creations for the theatre were Cora Laparcerie's costumes in *Le Minaret* in 1913, *Aphrodite* in 1914 and, in the cinema in 1923, Georgette Leblanc's costumes in Marcel L'Herbier's *L'Inhumaine*. From 1920 onwards, Rolf de Mare and his Swedish Ballet company were dressed by Paul Cohn, Jeanne Lanvin, Steinlen, Jean Hugo, Fernand Léger, Fujita, Giorgio de Chirico...

Prominent designers have often been commissioned to produce costumes for ballet in more recent years. Who could forget Christian Lacroix's extravagant, brightly coloured dresses for Mikhail Baryshnikov's American Ballet Theatre revival of *Gaîté Parisienne*, seen in London in 1990? The same year, when asked to costume one of William Forsythe's ballets, Issey Miyake chose simple designs, with permanent pleating, anticipating his Pleats Please collection.

Crossover between art and fashion

In 1913 the Russian abstract painter Sonia Delaunay, 'the grande dame of colour', started to create eccentric, brightly coloured clothes, which she called *les robes simultanées* (simultaneous dresses), putting together a wide assortment of fabrics in unexpected ways. In 1921, in a big flat in the boulevard Malesherbes in Paris, which was studio, home and couture house all in one, Delaunay dressed such prestigious clients as Nancy Cunard and the actresses Gloria Swanson and

Gabrielle Dorziat. She also designed spectacular clothes for Jacques Heim, and costumes for the theatre and the cinema. Elsa Shiaparelli also had close links with the world of art, and commissioned Salvador Dalí, Christian Bérard and Jean Cocteau to design fabrics and accessories. She was influenced in her work by Cubism and Surrealism.

Coco Chanel's costumes for cinema

Well before she dressed Delphine Seyrig in her famous little suits for the film *Last Year at Marienbad* in 1961, Coco Chanel had her first success with a very simple straw hat worn by Gabrielle Dorziat in *Bel-Ami* in 1912. She also created costumes for Génica Athanasiou in a brown wool cape for Dulim's *Antigone* in 1922. Knitted striped swimsuits for the dancers in *Blue Train* in 1924, and, for *Œdipus Rex* in 1937, she wrapped Jean Marais' sculptural body in strips of cloth which 'indecency' caused quite a scandal...

Costumes better than the films themselves

Costume designs for films have sometimes been far more memorable than the films themselves. The obscure French film *Qui êtes vous Polly Magoo?*, created by the photographer William Klein, would probably have been forgotten altogether were it not for its brilliant costumes. The clothes designed by, among others, Elsa Schiaparelli, for *Moulin Rouge* (1952) stood out in what was otherwise a rather mediocre film. *My Fair Lady* (1964) was a treat for the eye with its costumes by Cecil Beaton, particularly in the almost monochrome Ascot scene. Beaton, who had primarily worked as a photographer, had established himself as a designer with *Gigi* in 1958. For each film, he received an Academy Award. Another British designer who worked in the cinema was Norman Hartnell.

Designers inspired by art

Emilio Pucci admits that he drew inspiration for the fabrics he made in 1960 from the works of the Futurist painter Giacomo Balla. In 1966, Yves Saint Laurent was the first to renew contact with the world of art by creating a Pop

Dress by Ben Vautier 'I am quite naked underneath', 1984, for Jean-Charles de Castelbajac.

Art collection, inspired by Andy Warhol, Roy Lichtenstein and Tom Wesselmann, followed by regular homage to his favourite painters – the Mondrian dress in 1965, Velázquez in 1977, Picasso in 1979, David Hockney in 1987, the Cubists in 1988... In 1993, Jean-Paul Gaultier's trompe l'œil 'naked body' dress was obviously influenced by Magritte's *La Philosophie dans le boudoir*, and Comme des garçons in 1996 were evidently inspired by Matisse. Romeo Gigli has always claimed that the old master paintings in the Italian museums, where he was taken by his mother, inspired him to find the exceptional variety of colours used in his designs.

Art and fashion in the street

Throughout the 20th century, the constant exchanges between art and fashion have become a genuine dialogue. Clothes have become an excuse for mentioning works of art, and in reply, artists have integrated fashion into their subject matter. Some designers have become gallery directors; others make clothes like sculptures and exhibit them in museums of contemporary art. Clothes have acquired the status of works of art in their own right. There is no escaping from this. Couturiers and artists will always be associated, because they are interested in the same things. It may be the wonders of nature, the architect dictating the couturier's lines, the couturier paying homage to a dead painter, or contemporary artists who want to see their works walking down the street.

COMME DES GARÇONS

Rei Kawakubo, who launched the company Comme des garçons, set up in Paris in 1981, and became involved with the contemporary art world by inviting one artist every year to create an original work on the theme of the new collection. Bernard Faucon, Cindy Sherman and Daniel Buren took part in the experiment and created works in situ for the main shop in Tokyo. 'The most important thing when you are working in collaboration is that the artist should understand the theme of the collection. He must have a perfect grasp of what I am trying to say through the medium of this collection. It is the collection which defines the market that follows,' stated Rei Kawabuko (Art Press, special issue no. 18, Art et Mode 1997).

AGNÈS B.

Between 1981 and 1991, this designer, who was passionate about contemporary art, was behind Six (sixth sense), a magazine devoted to artists which accompanied each of her collections. Agnès b. has been involved in various activities and is interested in both the stylised and humanitarian aspects of contemporary art. She opened a bookshop and gallery in 1984, and soon became one of the prominent personalities in the field of contemporary art. A former art student, she has always maintained a privileged relationship with the art world. As well as her activities as a gallery owner, she publishes, in collaboration with Christian Boltanski and Hans-Ulrich Obrist, a magazine devoted to artists. Artistic creation also has a place of honour in her shops through T-shirts made by such artists as Rafael Gray, Aurèle Ganaes-Torres and Cyril Mariaux.

MARTIN MARGIELLA

The couturier Martin Margiella, who set up in 1988, explores the origins and authentic character of clothing. In 1997 the Museum Boijmans van Beuningen in Rotterdam devoted an exhibition to him and presented a collection of 'culture' clothes, full of different fungi, bacteria, yeasts and moulds, which transformed the textures, colours and feel of the textiles.

Our buying habits

The end of the 20th century saw significant changes in the fortunes of the various retail outlets for women's clothes in Britain. The majority of retail sales were by specialist chains, well-known names such as Dorothy Perkins, River Island, Etam and Benetton, with outlets in the high streets of most major towns and cities. Department stores were increasing their market share, at the expense of 'variety stores' – smaller high-street retailers selling a range of goods including clothing. Discount stores showed increased sales, but falling profits. Mail order was becoming less popular for buying clothes, partly because high-street chains had become more competitive, but partly because consumers had more money to spend, and were less likely to need credit. The independent retailers were also being squeezed out by the chains, being unable to compete on prices.

Women's clothing budgets

Price remained the major factor influencing consumer demand, but there was also a growing emphasis on quality. Generally, younger women tended to look for the cheaper clothes, and regarded fashion as more important than quality, but older women were demanding higher quality of both goods and service in shops. The most commonly purchased items were 'essentials' – skirts, dresses, trousers and knitwear. Perhaps surprisingly, skirts and dresses were now more popular than trousers and jeans, but this was due in part to the increasing numbers of women working and needing to dress reasonably smartly.

Who are the women doing the buying?

An ageing population, due to a lower birth rate and higher life expectancy, meant an inevitable change in buying habits. The largest growth of female population at the end of the 20th century was in the range of 35–44 years, with a decline in those aged 15–34. Fortunately for the fashion industry, it was clear that women of all ages – not just the young – were now demanding fashionable clothes. Retailers were beginning to appreciate a new phenomenon – that of older women returning to work after bringing up children, the so-called 'empty-nesters'. These women now had higher incomes and fewer family commitments, and were thus able to spend more on non-necessity items, such as the latest fashions. There had always been risks in catering solely for the young consumer, owing to the fickleness of fashion, and the increased spending power of older women now encouraged a change of emphasis.

Women's size and shape

In the late 1990s, the store group Debenhams commissioned a study from Nottingham Trent University to find out if the ready-to-wear clothes sold to women were suitable for their sizes and shapes. The results, achieved by accurately measuring 2,500 women with digital technology, proved surprising. In the previous 17 years it was found that women had put on an average of 4 kg (9 lb) in weight and that 40 per cent were wearing different sized tops and bottoms. Only a third were wearing the appropriate size. The average woman increases a dress size every 10 to 15 years, but she gradually loses height, and so her overall proportions and shape are altered. Debenhams were prompted to adjust their silhouette for all women's sizes as a result of the study.

Menswear: still the poor relation?

Although expenditure on menswear showed signs of increasing in the late 1990s, it was still way below that of womenswear. Men have been traditionally more reluctant clothes shoppers than women, but certain factors were beginning to change this. The main shift in buying habits had come about through casualwear becoming more acceptable and replacing the formal in many men's wardrobes. Many workplaces were now tolerating casualwear, and even encouraging it with the American practice of 'Dress Down Friday' being adopted in some offices. The traditional suit for work, always a major item of expenditure, was now no longer always necessary, and so men had more money to spend on other items of clothing. Another factor encouraging men to spend more on clothes has been the growth in the sports culture. Sports shops now take a significant share of the clothing market, and sportswear, however functional, is now seen as desirable casualwear. Men's choice of clothing remains more limited than that of women, but retailers are beginning to recognise that the new conditions in the clothing market for men mean that there are opportunites for expansion.

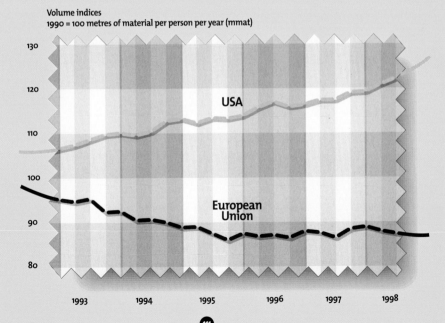

Consumption textiles/clothing

Volume indices
1990 = 100 metres of material per person per year (mmat)

Test your fashion knowledge

1 Who was the first couturier to launch a perfume? Charles Frederick Worth, Paul Poiret or Coco Chanel?

2 When did the first bikini appear?

3 Who started prêt-à-porter in France? Pierre Cardin, Jean-Claude Weill or Jacques Griffe?

4 Who was the first couturier to label his garments? Worth, Charles Redfern or Jacques Doucet?

5 Who won an Oscar for the costumes in the film *My Fair Lady*? Cecil Beaton, Yves Saint Laurent or Christian Dior?

6 Who claimed to have liberated women from their corsets? Coco Chanel, Paul Poiret or Edward Henry Molyneux?

7 Who perfected the first synthetic fibre? Du Pont, Courtaulds or Rhône Poulenc Textile?

8 Who invented the waspie? Christian Dior, Marcel Rochas or Jean-Paul Gaultier?

9 When did nylon stockings first appear?

10 Who invented lace tights? Mary Quant, Vivienne Westwood or Chantal Thomass?

11 Where does Paul Smith have his headquarters? London, Paris or Nottingham?

12 Who was the first Japanese couturier to open a couture house in Paris? Yohji Yamamoto, Kenzo or Rei Kawakubo?

13 Who was the first couturier to organise a European tour with his models to present his fashions? Redfern, Paul Poiret or Robert Piguet?

14 Who invented the tailored suit? Coco Chanel, Redfern or Alix?

15 Who became creative director at Dior in 1996? Alexander McQueen, John Galliano or Issey Miyake?

16 Who set up the first trend consultancy?

17 In which year was the first department store founded?

18 Which artist inspired Paul Poiret's Oriental designs? Paul Cézanne, Pablo Picasso or Léon Bakst?

19 Who invented the miniskirt? André Courrèges, Mary Quant or Yves Saint Laurent?

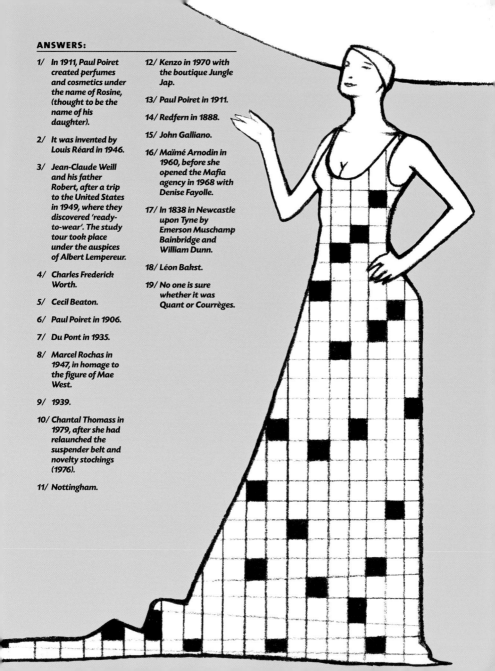

ANSWERS:

1/ In 1911, Paul Poiret created perfumes and cosmetics under the name of Rosine, (thought to be the name of his daughter).

2/ It was invented by Louis Réard in 1946.

3/ Jean-Claude Weill and his father Robert, after a trip to the United States in 1949, where they discovered 'ready-to-wear'. The study tour took place under the auspices of Albert Lempereur.

4/ Charles Frederick Worth.

5/ Cecil Beaton.

6/ Paul Poiret in 1906.

7/ Du Pont in 1935.

8/ Marcel Rochas in 1947, in homage to the figure of Mae West.

9/ 1939.

10/ Chantal Thomass in 1979, after she had relaunched the suspender belt and novelty stockings (1976).

11/ Nottingham.

12/ Kenzo in 1970 with the boutique Jungle Jap.

13/ Paul Poiret in 1911.

14/ Redfern in 1888.

15/ John Galliano.

16/ Maïmé Arnodin in 1960, before she opened the Mafia agency in 1968 with Denise Fayolle.

17/ In 1838 in Newcastle upon Tyne by Emerson Muschamp Bainbridge and William Dunn.

18/ Léon Bakst.

19/ No one is sure whether it was Quant or Courrèges.

Universities, colleges, schools of fashion, and museums

Universities and colleges offering courses in fashion design and related subjects, including management in the fashion industry, and technology.

This is not an exhaustive list, and further information is available at libraries. Entry requirements vary: most fashion degree courses will require a minimum of 5 GCSE passes, 2 'A' Level passes (or equivalent), and a foundation course in art and design. Work experience in a relevant area is an advantage, but not usually a requirement. Mature students will sometimes be accepted on the basis of a portfolio. For some courses, for example in fashion management or journalism, a portfolio is not relevant. Colleges are looking for fashion awareness, enthusiasm for learning, independence, and a real passion for their chosen career. Bear in mind also that there are courses specifically relating to individual professions within the fashion industry, and others that are more general in scope. Some will aim to give graduates a practical base, and encourage the creation of designs that are marketable, either at the high or low end of the market, while others will be more theoretical. Many prominent designers have come into the fashion industry after studying art-based subjects and it may be more useful in the long run to look for a course that will give a good grounding in art and design, before deciding which branch of the industry that you want to be involved in. There will most probably be plenty of time to make up your mind about where you want to start your career in fashion later. The industry is extensive, and you may find that you begin a course believing you know what you want to achieve, and end up being diverted into a completely different branch.

Prospective students have different criteria for deciding where to study. Some are attracted by a college's reputation and whether a famous designer once studied there. Some colleges are therefore oversubscribed, and competition for places is fierce, but don't be put off if you are rejected – many less well-known colleges offer excellent courses. Who knows, you may turn out to be a famous designer in the future and put your college on the map!

UNIVERSITIES COLLEGES AND ART SCHOOLS

LONDON COLLEGE OF FASHION
20 John Princes Street
London
W1G 0BJ
Tel. 020 7514 7579
Fax 020 7514 7560.

CENTRAL ST MARTINS COLLEGE OF ART AND DESIGN
Southampton Row
London
WC1B 4AP
Tel. 020 7514 7027

ROYAL COLLEGE OF ART
Kensington Gore
London
SW7 2EU
Tel. 020 7590 4444

THE ROYAL SCHOOL OF NEEDLEWORK
Apartment 12A
Hampton Court Palace
Surrey
KT8 9AU
Tel. (020) 8943 1432

BRETTON HALL COLLEGE
West Bretton
Wakefield
West Yorkshire
WF4 4LG
Tel. 01924 832 017

UNIVERSITY OF BRIGHTON
Mithras House
Lewes Road
Brighton
BN2 4AT
Tel. 01273 600900

UNIVERSITY OF CENTRAL ENGLAND
Perry Barr
Birmingham
B42 2SU
Tel. 0121 331 5595

UNIVERSITY OF CENTRAL LANCASHIRE
Preston
PR1 2HE
Tel. 01772 201201

CROYDON COLLEGE
Fairfield Campus
College Road
Croydon
CR9 1DX
Tel. 020 8656 5700

UNIVERSITY OF DERBY
Britannia Mill
Mackworth Road
Derby
DE22 3BL
Tel. 01332 622222

UNIVERSITY OF EAST LONDON
Docklands Campus
Royal Albert Way
London
E16 2QJ
Tel. 020 8223 7579

HERIOT-WATT UNIVERSITY
Riccarton
Edinburgh
EH14 4AS
Tel. 0131451 3376

KENT INSTITUTE OF ART AND DESIGN
Fort Pitt
Rochester
Kent
ME1 1DZ
Tel. 01634 830022

MANCHESTER METROPOLITAN UNIVERSITY
Faculty of Art and Design
Department of Textiles/Fashion
Cavendish Building
Cavendish Street
Manchester
M15 6BG
Tel. 0161 247 3525

MIDDLESEX UNIVERSITY
White Hart Lane
London
N17 8HR
Tel. 020 8362 5000

NORTHBROOK COLLEGE SUSSEX
Union Place
Worthing
BN11 1LG
Tel. 01903 606001

UNIVERSITY COLLEGE NORTHAMPTON
Park Campus
Boughton Green Road
Northampton
NN2 7AL
Tel. 01604 735500

THE UNIVERSITY OF NORTHUMBRIA AT NEWCASTLE
Ellison Place
Newcastle upon Tyne
NE1 8ST
Tel. 0191 232 6002

NOTTINGHAM TRENT UNIVERSITY
Burton Street
Nottingham
NG1 4BU
Tel. 0115 848 6410

RAVENSBOURNE COLLEGE OF DESIGN AND COMMUNICATION
Walden Road
Chislehurst
Kent
BR7 5SN
Tel. 020 8289 4900

Addresses

READING COLLEGE AND SCHOOL OF ARTS AND DESIGN
Crescent Road
Reading
Berkshire
RG1 5RQ
Tel. 0118 967 5000

UNIVERSITY OF SALFORD
Adelphi Building
Peru Street
Salford
Greater Manchester
M3 6EQ
Tel. 0161 295 6095

SALISBURY COLLEGE
Southampton Road
Salisbury
Wiltshire
SP1 2LW
Tel. 01722 323711

SOMERSET COLLEGE OF ARTS AND TECHNOLOGY
Wellington Road
Taunton
TA1 5AX
Tel. 01823 283403

THE SURREY INSTITUTE OF ART AND DESIGN
Falkner Road
Farnham
Surrey
GU9 7DS
Tel. 01252 732233

UNIVERSITY INFORMATION CENTRE
Caerleon Campus
University of Wales College
Newport
NP18 3YH
Tel. 01633 432432

UNIVERSITY OF WESTMINSTER
309 Regent Street
London
W1R 8AL
Tel. 020 7911 5000

WINCHESTER SCHOOL OF ART
Park Avenue
Winchester
SO23 8DL
Tel. 01962 842500

YORK COLLEGE OF FURTHER AND HIGHER EDUCATION
Dringhouses
York
YO2 1UA
Tel. 01904 704141

MUSEUMS

ALBY LACE MUSEUM AND STUDY CENTRE
Cromer Road
Alby Hall
Norwich
NR11 7QE
Tel. 01263 768002

BUTTON MUSEUM AND BUTTON SHOP
Kyrle Street
Ross-on-Wye
HR9 7DB
Tel. 01989 566089

CENTRAL MUSEUM AND ART GALLERY (BOOT AND SHOE COLLECTION)
Guildhall Road
Northampton
Tel. 01604 238548

FASHION RESEARCH CENTRE
4 Circus
Bath
BA1 2EW
Tel. 01225 477752

MUSEUM OF COSTUME
Assembly Rooms
Bennett Street
Bath
BA1 2QH
Tel. 01225 477 000
www.museumofcostume.co.uk

GALLERY OF ENGLISH COSTUME
Platt Hall
Rusholme
Manchester
M14 5LL
Tel. 0161 224 5217

THE LACE CENTRE
Severn's Building
Castle Road
Nottingham
NG1 6AA
Tel. 0115 941 3539

MUSEUM OF COSTUME AND TEXTILES
51 Castlegate,
Nottingham
NG1 6AF
Tel. 0115 915 5555

SHAMBELLIE HOUSE MUSEUM OF COSTUME
New Abbey
Dumfries
Dumfries and Galloway
DG2 8HQ
Tel. 01387 850375

SCOTTISH TARTANS MUSEUM
39–41 Princes Street
Edinburgh
EH2 2BY
Tel. 0131 556 1252

SPRINGHILL
Moneymore
Magherafelt
Co. Londonderry
BT45 7NQ
Tel. 02879 748210

VICTORIA AND ALBERT MUSEUM
Department of Textiles
Furnishing and Dress
South Kensington
London
SW7 2RL
Tel. 020 7942 2000
www.vam.ac.uk

KENSINGTON PALACE
State Apartments and Royal
Ceremonial Dress Collection
London, W8 4PX
Tel. 020 7937 9561

MUSEUMS IN FRANCE

MUSÉE DE LA MODE ET DU TEXTILE
Union centrale des arts décoratifs
Palais du Louvre,
107 rue de rivoli,
Paris 1er
Tel. 0033 1 44 55 57 50
www.ucad.fr

MUSÉE DES TISSUS
34 rue de la Charité
F-69002 Lyon
Tel. 0033 4 78 38 42 00

MUSÉE DE LA MODE ET DU COSTUME
Musée Galliera
10 av. Pierre-1er-de-Serbie
75016
Paris
Tel. 00 33 1 47 20 85 23

MUSÉE CHRISTIAN-DIOR
Villa de la Rhumbs
504000
Granville
Tel. 00 33 2 33 61 48 21

MUSÉE DES BEAUX-ARTS ET DE LA DENTEL.LE
25 rue Richelieu
62100
Calais
Tel. 00 33 3 21 46 48 40

MUSEUMS IN ITALY

CENTRO STUDI DI STORIA DEL TESSUTO E DEL COSTUME
Santa Croce
1992 Salizada San Stae
Venice 30125
Tel. 0039 041 721798

PALAZZO PITTI - GALLERIA DEL COSTUME
Piazza Pitti, 1
Florence
Tel. 0039 055 2388 713

MUSEUMS IN NORTH AMERICA

BLACK FASHION MUSEUM
2007 Vermont Avenue
Washington, DC 20001
Tel. 001 202 667 0744

KENT STATE UNIVERSITY MUSEUM
http://dept.kent.edu/
museum
PO Box 5190,
Rockwell Hall
Kent
OHIO 44242-0001,
Tel. 001 330 672 3450

SCOTTISH TARTANS MUSEUM
86 East Main St.
Franklin, NC 28734,
Tel. 001 828 524 7472

ELIZABETH SAGE HISTORIC COSTUME COLLECTION
Memorial Hall E. 232
Indiana University
Bloomington ,
Indiana 47405 ,
Tel. 001 812 855 4627

COSTUME MUSEUM OF CANADA
www.costumemuseum.com
Dugald and The Forks,
Manitoba
Tel. 001 853 2166
or 001 947-1624

MUSEUMS IN BELGIUM

MUSEUM OF COSTUME AND LACE
Violette Street 4-6
1000 Brussels
Tel. 0032 2512 7709

Associations and Trade Unions

**BRITISH APPAREL &
TEXTILE
CONFEDERATION**
5 Portland Place
London
W1N 3AA
Tel 020 7636 7788
Fax 020 7636 7515

**BRITISH CHAMBERS OF
COMMERCE**
4 Westwood House
Westwood Business Park
Coventry
CV4 8HS
Tel 02476 694484
Fax 02476 695844

**BRITISH CLOTHING
INDUSTRY
ASSOCIATION LTD**
5 Portland Place
London
W1N 3AA
Tel 020 7636 7788
Fax 020 7636 7515

**BRITISH FASHION
COUNCIL**
5 Portland Place
London
W1N 3AA
Tel 020 7636 7788
Fax 020 7636 7515

AEEU
*Amalgamated Engineering
and Electrical Union*
Hayes Court,
West Common Road
Bromley
Kent
BR2 7AU
Tel 020 8462 7755
Fax 020 8315 8234
www.aeeu.org.uk

**BECTU
BROADCASTING,
ENTERTAINMENT,
CINEMATOGRAPH AND
THEATRE UNION**
111 Wardour Street
London
W1V 4AY
Tel 020 7437 8506
Fax 020 7437 8268
www.bectu.org.uk

GMB
22/24 Worple Road
London
SW19 4DD
Tel 020 8947 3131
Fax 020 8944 6552
www.gmb.org.uk

GULO
*General Union of Loom
Overlookers*
9 Wellington Street
St John's
Blackburn
BB1 8AF
Tel 01254 51760
Fax 01254 51760

**MSF
MANUFACTURING
SCIENCE FINANCE**
MSF Centre
33–37 Moreland Street
London
EC1V 8HA
Tel 020 7505 3000
Fax 020 7505 3030
www.msf.org.uk

**KFAT
NATIONAL UNION OF
KNITWEAR, FOOTWEAR
AND APPAREL TRADES**
55 New Walk
Leicester
LE1 7EB
Tel 0116 255 6703
Fax 0116 254 4406
Fax (press & research)
0116 255 4464
www.kfat.org.uk

**T&GWU
TRANSPORT AND
GENERAL WORKERS'
UNION**
Transport House
128 Theobald's Road
Holborn
London
WC1X 8TN
Tel 020 7611 2500
Fax 020 7611 2555
www.tgwu.org.uk

**USDAW
UNION OF SHOP,
DISTRIBUTIVE AND
ALLIED WORKERS**
Oakley
188 Wilmslow Road
Fallowfield
Manchester
M14 6LJ
Tel 0161 224 2804,
0161 249 2400
Fax 0161 257 2566
www.usdaw.org.uk

**UTW
UNION OF TEXTILE
WORKERS**
18 West Street
Leek
Staffordshire
ST13 8AA
Tel 01538 382068
Fax 01538 384270

Internet addresses

GENERAL

THE FASHION PAGE
www.fashionz.co.uk

**GRADUATE FASHION
WEEK**
www.gfw.org.uk

FASHIONDEX ONLINE
www.fashiondex.com

FRENCH FASHION GUIDE
www.frenchfashion.com

**FASHION SEARCH
ENGINE**
www.fashionbot.com

**A GUIDE TO DESIGNERS
AND SHOPS**
www.fashion-411.com

**A GUIDE TO BRITISH
FASHION**
*www.widemedia.com/
fashionuk*

www.style.com

www.fashion.net

FASHION MAGAZINES ONLINE

www.elle.com

www.marieclaire.com

www.vogue.com

www.vogue.co.uk

www.vogue.presse.fr

www.armaniexchange.com

http://lucire.com

www.hintmag.com

www.fashionfinds.com

www.lumiere.com

DESIGNERS AND COUTURIERS

www.christian-lacroix.fr

www.chanel.fr

www.courreges.fr

www.dior.com

www.isseymiyake.com

www.jpgaultier.fr

www.givenchy.fr

www.paulsmith.co.uk

www.viviennewestwood.com

www.zandrarhodes.com

www.alexandermcqueen.net

www.maryquant.co.uk

www.thomaspink.co.uk

www.robertocavalli.net

www.jermynstreet.com

Further reading

Some of the books listed below may be out of print but should be available at major libraries or through the British Library.

General

On the Edge. Images from 100 Years of Vogue (introduction by Kennedy Fraser), Random House, New York, 1992

Alison Adburgham, *Shops and Shopping 1800–1914*, George Allen and Unwin Ltd, London, 1964

Sarah E Braddock and Marie O'Mahony, *Techno Textiles. Revolutionary Fibres for Fashion and Design*, Thames and Hudson, London, 1998

Nancy Bradfield, *Costume in Detail: Women's Dress 1730–1930*, George C. Harrap & Co, London, 1981

Iris Brooke, *A History of English Costume*, Eyre Methuen, London, 1979

Georgina O'Hara Callan, *The Encyclopedia of Fashion*, Thames and Hudson, London, 1986

Georgina O'Hara Callan, *The Thames and Hudson Dictionary of Fashion and Fashion Designers*, Thames and Hudson, London, 1998

P. Earnshaw, *Lace in Fashion: from the Sixteenth to the Twentieth Centuries*, Batsford , London, 1985

Elizabeth Ewing, *History of Twentieth Century Fashion*, Batsford, London, 1992

Elizabeth Ewing, *Dress and Undress*, Batsford, London, 1978

Martin Harrison, *Appearances. Fashion Photography since 1945*, Jonathan Cape, London, 1991

Janey Ironside, *A Fashion Alphabet*, Michael Joseph, London, 1968

Eleanor Johnson, *Fashion Accessories*, Shire, Princes Risborough, 1994

James Laver, *A History of Fashion and Costume*, Thames & Hudson, London, 1990

James Laver, *Taste and Fashion*, George Harrap and Co, London, 1937

Elizabeth Leese, *Costume Design in the Movies*, Dover, New York, 1991

Joanna Mack and Steve Humphries, *The Making of Modern London 1939–1945. London at War*, Sidgwick and Jackson Ltd, London, 1985

Diane de Marly, *The History of Haute Couture 1850–1950*, B.T. Batsford, London, 1980

Colin McDowell, *McDowell's Directory of Twentieth Century Fashion*, Muller, London 1987

Anne Mountfield, *Clothes and Fashion*, Macmillan, Basingstoke, 1988

Jane Mulvagh, *Vogue History of 20th Century Fashion*, Viking, London, 1988

David Price, "Introduction: Society, the Arts ... and Ladies' Underwear" in *Cancan!*, Cygnus Arts, London, 1998

Brian Reade, *The Dominance of Spain* (*Costume of the Western World* series), George G. Harrap and Company Ltd, London, 1951

Aileen Ribeiro, *Dress and Morality*, B.T. Batsford, London, 1986

Melissa Richards, The Birth of the Bra in *Key Moments in Fashion*, Hamlyn, London, 1998

Julian Robinson, *Fashion in the 40s*, Academy Editions, London, 1980

Valerie Steele, *Paris Fashion. A Cultural History*, Oxford University Press, New York and Oxford, 1988

John M. Turnpenny, *Fashion Design and Illustration*, Hutchinson, London, 1981

R. Turner Wilcox, *A Dictionary of Costume*, B.T. Batsford, London, 1970

Personalities

Richard Avedon, *The naked and the dressed – 20 years of Versace, Richard Avedon and Versace* London: Jonathan Cape 1998

François Baudot, *Paul Poiret* London: Thames and Hudson 1997

François Baudot, *Chanel* London: Thames and Hudson 1996

François Baudot, *Christian Lacroix* London: Thames and Hudson 1996

Pierre Berge and Grace Mirabella, *Yves Saint Laurent* London: Thames and Hudson 1997

Meredith Etherington-Smith and Jeremy Pilcher, *The 'It' Girls. Lucy Lady Duff Gordon, the couturière Lucile and Elinor Glyn romantic novelist* London: Hamilton 1986

France Gran, *Comme des Garçons* London: Thames and Hudson 1998

Valérie Guillaume, *Courrèges* London: Thames and Hudson 1998

Mark Holborn, *Issey Miyake* Cologne: Taschen 1995

Marie-Andre Jouve, *Balenciaga* London: Thames and Hudson 1997

Diane de Marly, *Worth. Father of Haute Couture* London: Elm Tree Books 1980

Richard Martin and Harold Koda, *Christian Dior* New York: Harry N. Abrams Inc 1997

Catherine McDermott, *Vivienne Westwood* London: Carlton 1999

Colin McDowell, *Galliano* London: Phoenix Illustrated 1998

Colin McDowell, *Jean Paul Gaultier* London: Cassell and Co 2000

Jane Mulvagh, *Vivienne Westwood – an unfashionable life* London: HarperCollins 1998

Mary Quant, *Quant by Quant* London: Pan Books 1967

Zandra Rhodes and Anne Knight, *The Art of Zandra Rhodes* London: Jonathan Cape 1980

Charles Spencer, *Léon Bakst* London: Academy Editions 1973

Hugo Vickers, *Cecil Beaton. The Authorised Biography* London: Wiedenfeld and Nicolson 1985

Janet Wallach, *Chanel – Her Style and her Life* London: Mitchell Beazley 1999

Palmer White, *Elsa Schiaparelli* London: Aurum Press Ltd 1995

ACETATE

Artificial fibre made from cellulose, often used for lining jackets.

BIOTEXTILES

Scientific treatment of textiles to combat moulds, bacteria and mites.

BOBBIN

Small rod of decoratively turned wood used in lace and braid-making.

BUTTONHOLE STITCH

Similar to blanket stitch, used to edge buttonholes to prevent fraying, and also used decoratively.

CAPELINE

A woollen, loose-textured hood worn by women

CASAQUE

In the 16th and 17th centuries, a gentleman's coat. Nowadays a jockey's colours.

CHAIN STITCH

Embroidery stitches that overlap and give the effect of the links in a chain.

CHINÉ

Having a mottled pattern.

CHITON

Short tunic worn next to the skin by the ancient Greeks.

CORSET

Feminine undergarment used to hold in the waist and stomach; boned bodice, worn outside the dress or forming part of it.

CRINOLINE

Framework of hoops, over which ladies wore very full skirts in the mid-19th century.

CROCHET HOOK

Rigid metal implement with a curved tip, used for crochet or embroidery.

DOUBLET

Man's garment, made of rich fabric and padded, covering the upper part of the body. Worn from the 15th to the 17th centuries.

ECHIGNOL

Small piece of machinery that turns on an axle to create skeins of silk.

ELASTANE
Elastic fibre which gives materials extra stretch.

FARTHINGALE
Cone-shaped skirt, which came in from Spain at the end of the 15th century, held out by a frame of wood or whalebone covered with cloth.

FIBULA
Antique metal pin or brooch for fastening garments.

FINISHING
All the processes which give the fabric its final appearance.

FRAISE
Large stiffened lace collar, fashionable in the 16th and 17th centuries.

FROGGING
Braid used to make fastenings for a garment.

GOFFERING
Also known as crimping. Printing motifs in relief, using a hot iron.

GUÊPIÈRE
Small lightweight corset made to produce a narrow waist, also known as the 'waspie'.

GUTTA
Fabric glue of vegetable origin.

HAUTS-DE-CHAUSSE
Men's breeches, as worn from the end of the Middle Ages to the 15th century.

HENNIN
A tall cone-shaped hat, also known as the steeple-hat, worn in the 15th century.

HOUPPELANDE
Long coat with sleeves, originally worn by shepherds.

JABOT
A bunch of lace attached to the shirt, the ancestor of the tie.

JUSTAUCORPS
Kind of doublet with skirts or tails and a narrow waist and sleeves, popular in the 17th century.

LAMINOIR
Machine with steel rollers used in braid making.

MICROFIBRES
Fibres of less than 1 decitex (compared with 3 decitex for a normal synthetic fibre).

MODEL
An original design created as a pattern, from which copies can be produced.

MODÉLISTE

Term used both for a fashion designer and for the person who creates the first three-dimensional model of a garment from the two-dimensional drawing.

OVERLOCKER

Machine that can overstitch edges or join two fabrics edge to edge.

PAILLETTES

Similar to sequins; small, thin pieces of shiny metal or plastic sewn onto garments.

PANNIER

Very full underskirt with a metal or wooden frame.

PATCH

Small piece of black silk, which women stuck on their faces or their décolleté in the 17th and 18th centuries to show off the whiteness of their skin.

PLUMASSIER

A person who makes feathers into decorations for clothes.

POUF

Flounce of gathered material, which can be added to a dress to change the look.

POULAINE

Shoe with a long, pointed toe, worn in the 14th and 15th centuries.

PRESSER-FOOT

Part of a sewing machine that keeps the fabric in place and guides it through. The needle passes between the two prongs.

PROTOTYPE

The first completed version of a garment or object.

REFLEXITE°

Reflective material used in road signs and on protective clothing

RHOVYL°

Antibacterial chlorofibre produced by Rhovyl.

ROUET

Machine that twists fabric to form a cord and winds it onto a bobbin.

SCOTCHLITE°

Made by 3M. Glass fibres in resin applied to a fabric (65% polyester and 35% cotton), giving it reflective properties.

SLASH

Opening cut into a fabric to show a different coloured lining.

SPARTERIE

Natural fibre material used to make the framework of a hat.

SPENCER

A short jacket.

SPINNING

All the operations which turn raw fibres into yarn.

STOCKMAN

Tailor's dummy, named after Fred Stockman, who made the first mass-produced studio dummies that were faithful to the female figure.

STRASS

Paste for making false gems, named after its inventor Josef Strasser.

TOILE

Unbleached cotton fabric used to make the first fabric version of a pattern or model.

VELCRO°

American company which patented the strip fastening which works by interlocking hundreds of tiny hooks.

WASPIE

Corset with suspenders, created by Marcel Rochas in 1945, pushing up the bust and giving a very narrow 'wasp' waist.

WEAVE

Means the way the warp and weft are set up on a loom.

WHALEBONE

Flexible metal or plastic rod used to stiffen corsets.

Calender of events

LONDON

February
London Fashion Week
London Fashion Council
0870 429 4318
http://londonfashionweek.co.uk

Late September: summer collections

PARIS

Middle of March: autumn collections
Early October: summer collections

Chambre Syndicale De La Coutre
Tel: 0033 1 42 66 64 44

Interselection
May and November
Parc des expositions de Paris-Nord Villepinte
37-39, rue de Neuilly
Tel.: 0033 1 48 63 30 30

Salon des Créateurs
March and October
Carrousel du Louvre
Jardin des Tuilleries
Tel.: 0033 1 49 09 60 00

HONG KONG

Hong Kong Fashion Weeks
July and January
Hong Kong Convention and Exhibition Center
Hong Kong Trade Development Council
www.tdc.org.hk

MILAN

Middle of March: autumn collections
Early October: summer collections

Camera Nationale Della Moda Italiana
Tel: 0039 02 4800 8286

NEW YORK

Beginning of April
Mid September: summer collections

Council of Fashion Designers of America
Tel: 001 212 302-1821

Contents

Fact ⟩⟩ 2–12
Fun facts and quick quotes

Discover ⟩⟩ 13–40

Look ⟩⟩ 41–62

Backstage at a fashion show

In practice ⟩⟩ 63–92

Find out ⟩⟩ 93–125

Credits

P.15, AKG Paris, (Werner Forman). – **P.16,** AKG Paris. – **P.19,** DR. – **P.20,** AKG Paris. – **P.23,** Photothèque Hachette. – **P.23,** Boyer. – **P24,** Photothèque Hachette. – **P.27,** Photothèque Hachette. – **P.28,** AKG Paris. – **P.31,** The Bridgeman Art Library. – **P.32,** Getty One Stone. **P.35,** Rue des Archives. – **P.36,** Archives Versace (Dan Lecca). – **P.39,** Archives Hanae Mori (Olivier Claisse). **P.42 to 45,** Ludovic Carème. – **P.46,** Rapho (G. Uferas). – **P47 to 56,** Ludovic Carème. – **P.57 to 62,** Rapho (G.Uferas). – **P.70–71,** Trend notebooks from the Peclers Agency, Gilbert Nencioli. – **P.72–89,** Jean-Charles de Castelbajac, Wag. – **P.78–81,** Gilbert Nencioli. – **P.82–83,** Wag. – **P.84–85,** Gilbert Nencioli. – **P.90 to 92,** Wag, Gilbert Nencioli. – **P.95,** Creapole. – **P.97,** Thierry Elfezzani. – **P.98,** Levi's. – **P.99,** petit Bateau. – **P.100,** Rue des Archives. – **P.101,** Repetto. – **P.102,** Jean-Noël Reichel, *Des photographies et le cardigan pression*, Galeries du Jour. – **P.103,** Ben Simon, Archives, Converse. – **P.104 to 107,** Thierry Elfezzani. – **P.108,** Jean-Pierre Peersman, *JC de Castelbajac Album*, Michel Aveline, Editor. – **P.111,** Wag. – **P.112 to 125,** Thierry Elefzzani.

Acknowledgements

Jean-Charles de Castelbajac (Supernatural Collection, winter 2000–2001, ready-to-wear), Jean-Philippe Vaucler, Director of Daroux-Vaucler, School of Modelling, Laetitia Saint Olive, Textile designer, Marie-Andrée Jouve, Head of Archives at Balenciaga, Sébastien de Diesbach, Director of Promostyl, Domonique Peclers, Director of Peclers-Paris, Anne-Claude Georges, Buyer for Printemps, Lionel Guerin, Director of the Féderation française du vêtement, Du Pont de Nemours, Philippe Fort, Musée de la mode de la ville de Paris, Palais Galliera, Petit Bateau, Agnès b., Lacoste, Pierre at Anne Boyé.

Sources: P.2, l'Etudiant, Guide des métiers 1999; Fédération française du prêt-à-porter féminin – P.3, Fédération française de la couture; CIRFS; Les cahiers de l'ONISEP, no. 13, April 1999; Du Pont de Nemours – P.6, Quid 1999 – P.7, Les cahiers de l'ONISEP, no. 13, April 1999 – P.11, Les cahiers de l'ONISEP, no. 13, April 1999; CETH – P.110–111, Fédération française du prêt-à-porter féminin, 1999.